Fort Plain & Fort Plank

Two Fort Plain Revolutionary War Forts

In the words of those who served.

Compiled by A. J. Berry
for The Fort Plain Museum
and Historical Park

TABLE OF CONTENTS

Pension Applications

*We must be careful stewards of our history
and not rewrite the past to suit our wishes.*

Foreword

This book contains some of the pension applications of the men who served in Fort Plain and in Fort Plank, told in their words. End Notes are by James F. Morrison, Sr., unless otherwise noted.

There were several other forts in the surrounding area and in the future perhaps they will be studied as well.

The image of Fort Plain on the front cover was constructed by Len Tantillo from archaeological and historical evidence.

Excerpt is from the pension of Richard Putman.

Many pensions contain reference to both of the forts. To date I have transcribed over 6,000 of the pensions from New York State.

What James F. Morrison does after the transcription is of great value to those who seek the truth. Just because a man claimed he served, doesn't mean he did. The depositions were some 50 years after the service and the men were eager to qualify for a pension. Many factors were at play here, the biggest one being old age and loss of memory, with a close factor of wanting to qualify for a pension. Careful research authenticates the real service of the men by using other historical documents such as muster rolls, pay rolls, regimental records, other pension applications, and so forth. Sometimes the veteran's claims are unfounded. James F. Morrison's work is a true gift to posterity. Since he is a two fingered typist, I do that work and the web work to post the pensions on line. As Jim says, "Joyce, it takes two of us, without either one of us, it wouldn't get done."

In the next year NY should be completed and from there we will look at the other states because many served in NY from the Continental Army.

AJ Berry

Fort Plain/Fort Rensselaer
By Norman J. Bollen

The village of Fort Plain was originally named for an important military outpost in the Revolutionary War. It began, like literally dozens of other forts on the New York frontier, as a refuge for local inhabitants in times of danger. After the 1777 Battle of Oriskany had decimated the Tryon County Militia the Mohawk Valley was unable to defend itself. Raids occurred on frontier settlements throughout 1778 forcing the abandonment of homes and farms in the region. The Cherry Valley Massacre in November was considered the worst of the year's attacks forcing Congress to act against the Loyalist Indian tribes of western New York. During the fall and spring of 1779, Fort Plain was built as a refuge for local residents and evacuees from the Cherry Valley area. By 1780 General Van Rensselaer had decided to make the tiny fort his headquarters and the fort was thus renamed Fort Rensselaer. The summer of 1780 brought the "Burning of the Valleys", a devastating series of raids led by Sir John Johnson. Johnson and his chief lieutenants, Walter Butler and Joseph Brant moved through the valley burning homes, farms and fields. In August of that year a raiding party surprised the Canajoharie District surrounding Fort Plain but failing to take the fort. They burned the Canajoharie Reformed Church, then located on the adjacent Sand Hill. Almost the entire garrison was away escorting supplies to Fort Stanwix. Women and children in the area had fled into the fort and donned men's uniforms to walk the walls and give the impression of a strong defense. The ruse worked and the fort was saved.

After the Battles of Stone Arabia and Klock's field, Marinus Willett, the hero of Fort Stanwix, had been chosen to replace General Van Rensselaer. It was Willett who led the attack against the British camps outside of Fort Stanwix and later slipped through the enemy's lines to come down the valley for help. Willett also made Fort Plain his headquarters and began improving the fortifications there. He added an exterior Blockhouse about 400 yards northwest of the main fort effectively transforming the entire hilltop into a much larger fortified position. The space between the fort and the blockhouse filled with additional soldiers, displaced families and supportive services such as a cookhouse and blacksmith shop. While Willett had clearly preferred the name "Fort Plain" out of respect for the local citizens he was under orders to use the name Fort Rensselaer in all official correspondence.

In July of 1781 scouting parties from Fort Rensselaer had discovered the camp of a Loyalist raiding party at present day Sharon Springs. Willett immediately assembled 140 men to march all night to surprise the enemy. Under the Colonel's daring leadership they attacked and defeated an enemy force twice their size. Again in October of that year Colonel Willett attacked and defeated a much larger British force at the Battle of Johnstown.

In February 1783 Willett was entrusted with what must be the final mission of the American Revolution. General Washington asked Willett to lead an assault team to capture Fort Ontario in Oswego. The mission was kept secret and no one knew the destination until the last minute. The mission only failed when the guides became confused in the dark and the element of surprise was lost. The fort remained in British hands for another 13 years.

In July of that year General Washington decided to visit the upstate area before he returned home to Virginia. On July 28th Washington reviewed the troops at Fort Rensselaer and received a welcome worthy of the new Commander in Chief. Using Fort Rensselaer as his base the Commander-in-Chief visited forts up river as far as Rome, NY and south as far as Cherry Valley and Otsego Lake. On August 2nd Washington returned again to Fort Rensselaer to commemorate the Aug 2nd Canajoharie Raid with the officials of Tryon County in a great celebratory banquet at the fort.

The Strategy at Fort Plain

Prior to 1781 a number of outposts both north and south of the valley were constructed to monitor the approach of enemy raiding parties. Fort Plank, located several miles south of the river and west of Fort Plain/Rensselaer was originally constructed on the property of Frederick Plank almost a year before the construction of Fort Plain. Its high ground location afforded a perfect view of the Cherry Valley hills and southerly approaches. The fort was an important supply outpost from 1778-1780 when most of its inventory was moved to Fort Plain/Rensselaer, a safer location much closer to the river. In 1781, with the Continental Army leaving the frontier to join Washington at Yorktown, Fort Schuyler was closed and positions were consolidated with Fort Rensselaer as the new headquarters and supply depot for the western Mohawk Frontier. Fort Plank continued as one of many valuable satellite outposts that would comprise the valley's defensive strategy for the remainder of the war.

The site of Fort Plain was chosen both for its defendable hilltop and strategic location in the valley. From the hilltop one could observe the Mohawk River in both directions and also the Otsquago Creek, which runs south to meet the headwaters of the Susquehanna River System. It was at this point on the river that General James Clinton brought his 2000 man army to head south to Otsego Lake and down the Susquehanna River to join General Sullivan in their march to attack the Loyalist Indians of western New York. The fort hilltop itself was an almost impregnable position. Three sides of the hill are very steep and at the time were covered with sharpened brambles and thorn bushes called *"abates"*. The fourth side of the hill formed an isthmus, which was cut across by trenches and a defensive *Redoubt* designed by French Engineer Jean de Villefranche.

Fort Plain Today

The Fort Plain Museum began operation in 1961 as the Fort Plain Restoration with an emphasis on rebuilding Revolutionary War Fort Plain. At that time the museum began archaeological field work on the Fort Plain hilltop, unearthing 18th century period artifacts relating to the fort's history. On April 26, 1963 the museum received a "Provisional Charter" from the State of New York and a designation as a 501C3 not-for-profit educational institution. Archaeology continued in 1964 as additional sites relating to colonial Fort Plain/Fort Rensselaer were unearthed. In 1968 the organization received an "Absolute Charter" from the University of the State of New York Making the institution a permanent member of the museum community. Archaeological investigation and research continued in 1975 under the auspices of Wayne Lenig who excavated the site of the original fort's stockade. The exploration uncovered barracks buildings, a dining hall, officer's quarters, a small blockhouse and sentry posts.

During the 1980's and 90's the museum has developed exhibits on the different eras of history of the village of Fort Plain. Currently the museum's exhibits span the 17th, 18th and 19th centuries covering such topics as the Mohawk and Oneida Indians, German Palatines of the Mohawk, Victorian Era in the valley and the Erie Canal. Recently the Board of Directors decided the museum should refocus its efforts on the original colonial Fort Plain/Fort Rensselaer story. Research is again underway focusing on the fort's role in American history as the defender of the Mohawk Valley.

The museum property encompasses a park of approximately 75 acres and contains the following site and features:

- Excavated site of a 3 story square blockhouse
- Site of Revolutionary War Fort Plain/ Fort Rensselaer
- ¾ mile of original Otsquago Trail Road
- Foundation of Revolutionary War era bridge
- Site of two settlers cabins near the Otsquago Trail Road (presently not open to the public)
- Freshwater spring originally described as water supply to the fort
- Section of the Erie Canal (presently not open to the public)

- Stone farm house of David Lipe built in 1848
- Reconstructed farm house of Johannes Lipe ca. 1780
- Mill dam ca. 1860 (presently not open to the public)
- Site central cook house on fort hill
- Site of blacksmith shop which served the fort
- Site of Fort Rensselaer Redoubt & Crown works
- Remains of earthen trench works originally dug for defense of the hilltop

In 2009 the museum débuted new indoor and outdoor exhibits on Fort Plain's role in the Revolutionary War and the defense of the Mohawk Valley. The hilltop grounds are open daily from sunrise to sunset.

Pension Application for Thomas Campbell, Camble, Cammel
R.1646
State of New York
Madison County SS.

On this sixth day of October, personally appeared in open court before the Jude [sic] of the Court of Common Pleas in & for the County of Madison, aforesaid now sitting Thomas Campbell, a resident of the Town of Sullivan in the County of Madison & State of New York, aged sixty seven years on the 12th day of March last past, who being first duly sworn according to law doth on his oath make the following declaration, in order to obtain the benefit of the act of Congress passed June 7, 1832.

That he entered the service of the United States under the following named officers & served as herein stated.

That in the forepart of the month of August in the year 1781, he enlisted into the company of Captain Garret Putman, (1) belonging to the Regiment of Colo. Marinus Willett, for the term of four months. That he, at the time he entered the service then resided in the town of Florida in the County of Montgomery & State of New York, Victor Putman Lieutenant in the company & Gerret Newkirk ensign. (2) **That in the fore part of this enlistment, he was stationed at Fort Hunter, & in the latter part at Fort Plank, Fort Plain, & Fort Clyde, all situated upon the borders of the Mohawk River; in the state aforesaid. That this applicant was in the battle at Johnstown (3) in the County of Montgomery. That the battle took place in the month of October, 1781, but the day of the month this applicant from his own memory cannot state.**

That at the time of the battle he was stationed at Fort Plank aforesaid. That the day before the battle this applicant had been on a scouting party into the town of Sharon in the County of Schoharie, that he returned to Fort Plain aforesaid in the evening & started immediately for Johnstown & arrived at Johnstown in the afternoon of the next day—That after the said battle this applicant marched to the German Flatts upon the said Mohawk

River where he remained about two days & then returned to Fort Plank & remained there until he was discharged—That he received a written discharge from Major Throop (4) who belonged to the Regiment of Colo. Willett. That the discharge is lost. That he served the full term of his enlistment to wit, four months.

Capt. Moody (5) had command of a company of artillery, belonging to the Continental establishment, which was stationed at Fort Plain—Capt. Gross (6) was also stationed at Fort Plain, with a company of nine months men.

That this deponent does not recollect the names of any officers other than the ones above named, excepting Capt. Harrison. (7) Maj. Ross had command of the British forces at the Johnstown battle. This deponent further recollects that Maj. Rowley (8) was at the Johnstown Battle & had command of the New England troops—That he has no documentary evidence of his services & that he knows of no person whose testimony he can procure, who can testify to his service, other than what accompanys this declaration.

That in the year 1782 this deponent volunteered & entered the service at various & different times—Mostly into the company of militia commanded by Capt. McMaster; which was stationed or quartered at Fort McMaster, in the Town of Florida, aforesaid. Capt. McMaster's (9) company belonged to the regiment of Colo. Fisher, as this claimant believes—That his services in the year 1782 was confined to the summer & fall of that year That this claimant would be in actual service sometimes for a week or ten days & at other times more & sometimes less & then would return home & remain until he was called into service again—

This deponent cannot state more particularly the precise times, or the length thereof, but is positive that whole time, that his service in the summer & fall of the year 1782, would amount in the aggregate to four months & so states the facts to be—that this claimant received no written discharge from the company of Capt. McMaster—That at one time when this claimant was called out, within the fort above four months he, together with Capt. McMaster & the most of his company marched to Johnstown aforesaid & took a man by the name of Parker, (10) a spy, a prisoner, who was afterwards executed as a spy at Albany.

He hereby relinquishes every claim whatever to a pension or annuity except the present, & declares that his name is not on the pension roll of the agency of any state.

This claimant further swears that he was born in the town of Florida aforesaid on the 12th day of March 1767 as he has been informed by his parents & believes the same to be true.

That he has no record of his age.

That he was living in the Town of Florida aforesaid at the time & times when he entered the service—That since the Revolutionary War Thomas resided in the said Town of Florida, & in the town of Cherry Valley & in the Town of Sullivan aforesaid, where I now reside, & have resided for the space of twenty five years last past.

That I entered the service both under an enlistment & as a volunteer.

I cannot state the names of the regular officers who were with the troops when I served or the Continental & militia regiments, & the general circumstances of my service then or more particulars than I have herein before stated.

I received a written discharge from Maj. Throop. The discharge is lost.

I am known to Asa Cady, David Kennedy, Jonas Brown & Francis Hunt, persons who reside in my present neighborhood, & who can testify as to my character for veracity, & their belief of my services as a soldier of the revolution. (Signed) Thomas Campbell

Sworn to & subscribed this [blank] day of October 1834 before me. A. S. Sloan, Clk.

End Notes—R.1646—Thomas Campbell

1. Garret Putman was appointed Captain on April 27, 1781 in Lieutenant Colonel Commandant Marinus Willett's Regiment of New York State Levies. On Captain Putman's Receipt roll Thomas was owed £10. . 3. .4 which was never paid. FROM: Revolutionary War Rolls 1775-1783, Series M-246, Roll 78, Folder 173, National Archives, Washington, D.C.

2. Victor Putman and Garret Newkirk were appointed lieutenants on the same date and were assigned to Captain Putman's Company.

3. The Battle of Johnstown was fought on October 25, 1781.

4. Josiah Throop was appointed major on April 28, 1781 in Willett's Regiment.

5. Captain Andrew Moody of the Second Continental Artillery Regiment. Captain Moody and his company were stationed in the Mohawk Valley in 1781 and were in the Battle of Johnstown and some went with Willett in pursuit of Major John Ross and were in the skirmish at West Canada Creek on October 30, 1781.

6. Captain Lawrence Gross of Willett's Regiment and was also in the Battle of Johnstown.

7. Joseph Harrison was appointed captain on April 28, 1781 in Willett's Regiment.

8. Aaron Rowley was major of Colonel Elisha Porter's Regiment of the Massachusetts State Levies in 1781. Rowley was wounded in the leg at the Battle of Johnstown.

9. David McMaster was the Captain of the Sixth Company in Colonel Frederick Visscher's Third Regiment of Tryon County Militia. Thomas was only 14 in 1781 but his father must have had his father's permission to enlist as he was under 16 years of age. The only Campbells found in McMaster's Company as serving were John and Samuel as privates and Nathaniel as a sergeant.

10. John Parker. He lived in Philadelphia Bush which is now Perth, Fulton County, New York. Parker enlisted as a private on May 6, 1777 in the First Battalion of the King's Royal Regiment of New York commanded by Sir John Johnson.

Pension Application for John DeGraff (DeGraf)

S.28711

State of New York

County of Onondaga

On this twelfth day of September in the year of our Lord one thousand eight hundred and thirty two personally appeared at a court of Chancery held at Onondaga before Daniel Moseley Esq., Vice Chancellor of the 2nd Circuit now sitting John De Graff a resident of the Town of Camillus in said county aged seventy two years, who being first duly sworn according to law, doth on his oath make the following declaration in order to obtain the benefit of the act of Congress passed June 7th 1832.

That he was born in the then town, now City of Schenectady in said State in the year of our Lord one thousand seven hundred and sixty. That he has no record of his age except that contained in his family Bible which was burnt with his father's house. That he this claimant lived in said Town of Schenectady at the time he was called into the service of the United States. After the Revolutionary War closed, he moved to the Town of Amsterdam in the now County of Montgomery and resided there for the term of fifteen or sixteen years. Then moved to the fourth ward of the City of Schenectady, aforesaid, now Town of Glenville, lived there fifteen or sixteen years, thereupon moved to Schoharie where he lived about one year and about one year ago came to the said Town of Camillus where he now resides.

He entered the service of the United States under the following named officers and served as herein stated.

In the summer of the year one thousand seven hundred and seventy seven, he was enrolled as a private in a company of militia commanded by Captain John Mynderse (1) in the regiment whereof Abraham Wemple Esq. was colonel. His other company and field officers whom he recollects, were as follows, Lawrence Mynderse first Lieutenant, James H. Peek second Lieutenant and Abraham I. Truax, Ensign, Abraham Swits & Myndert Wemple, Majors. He continued to serve in said company whenever called upon until the termination of said war.

He was with the detachments of militia from said regiment that were from time to time ordered out, besides being out on several occasions as a scout and in small reconnoitering parties among the Tories and Indians. He served for a longer or shorter period every year of the war but how long he served each year, and at what particular military posts or forts, he cannot possibly recollect yet honestly and sincerely believes, that the time he served his country in the War of the Revolution exceeds four years –

He served in the year 1777 under Generals Schuyler, Gates and Arnold (2), for the term of three months at Fort Edward, Stillwater, and places in that vicinity, previous to and at the time of the surrender of General Burgoyne and his army to the American forces.

In the fall of the year 1778, one third of the militia of this state being ordered out, he was among the number that were stationed at Fort Paris in Stone Arabia. He was at that fort also on other occasions, he had likewise performed garrison duty at Fort Hunter, Fort Plank and Fort Plain; at Fort Plank he thinks in the fall of the year 1779. He has performed military duty different times at the lower and middle forts at Schoharie, Schenectady, and Cobles Kill. Was at the last named place immediately after it was destroyed by the Tories and British and assisted in burying the dead. He has also performed military service at Canajoharie, Palatine and Johnstown. Sir John Johnson having burnt all the buildings and destroyed the property of the Whigs at Caughnawaga (3), passed up the north side of the Mohawk River, and destroyed everything in his course, he was there with the militia in pursuit of Sir John Johnson. He was at Ballston (4) when it was burnt by the enemy in the year 1780. He was then under the command of Major Swits, and Major Michell (5) was at Beaverdam a place very much infested with Tories who made that a place of rendezvous. He assisted on one occasion in taking about one hundred of them prisoners.

A noted Tory by the name of Jo. Bettis was continually communicating intelligence to the enemy. Parties of militia were often out in pursuit of him and his associates. The claimant in company with others of the militia was several times in search of them, at Norman's Kill at the Heldebergh and at Ballston, he believes in the year 1782.

He knew Generals Schuyler, Van Rensselaer (6), and Gates, Colonel Van Schaick, Colonel Van Dyck and Captain Fink, Colonel Willett and many other officers besides those named in this declaration.

He never to his knowledge received any written discharge from the service, and is not aware that such discharges were at any time given to any of the members of his company, or in fact to any of the militia.

The following are the names of persons to whom he is known in his present neighborhood, and who can testify as to his character for veracity and their belief of his services as a soldier in the army of the revolution.

He has no documentary evidence, and knows of no persons other (then those whose testimony he has procured to verify above) now living whose testimony he can procure, who can testify to his service.

He hereby relinquishes every claim whatever to a pension or annuity except the present, and declares that his name is not on the pension roll of the agency of any state. (Signed with his mark) John DeGraff

Subscribed and Sworn to the day and year first aforesaid.
Daniel Moseley, Circuit Judge & Vice Chancellor.

End Notes—John DeGraff -- S.28711

1. Captain John Mynderse's (Mynderson, etc.) Company in Colonel Abraham Wemple's Regiment of Albany County Militia (Second Regiment). All of the other officers mentioned in this paragraph were as he states, in Colonel Wemple's Regiment.

2. General Philip Schuyler, Horatio Gates and Benedict Arnold all served in the Northern American Army.

3. Sir John Johnson with his British forces and Indian Allies burned Caughnawaga and the surrounding area on May 22, 1780.

4. Ball's Town (Now Ballston Spa area) was destroyed by British forces on October 17, 1780.

5. Major Andrew Mitchell was in Colonel Jacobus Van Schoonhoven's Regiment of Albany County Militia (Twelfth Regiment).

6. Brigadier General Robert Van Rensselaer, Colonel Goose Van Schaick and Lieutenant-Colonel Cornelius VanDyck both of the First New York Continental Regiment, Captain Andrew Fink of the First New York afterwards (1781-1783) as Brigade Major in Colonel Marinus Willett's Regiment of New York State Levies.

Pension Application for John Duesler
or Deusler, Tuesler, Tussler

W.16244

Declaration in order to obtain the benefit of the act of Congress passed June 7, 1832.

State of New York
Herkimer County SS.

On this twelfth day of February in the year of our Lord one thousand eight hundred and thirty three personally appeared in open court, before the Judges of the Court of Common Pleas of the County of Herkimer now sitting, John Duesler, a resident of the town of Danube in the County of Herkimer and State of New York, aged seventy five years on the twenty first day of August last past, who being first duly sworn according to law, doth on his oath make the following declaration in order to obtain the benefit of the act of Congress passed June 7, 1832.

That at the commencement of the Revolutionary War this deponent was a private in a company of Militia, commanded by Capt. Abraham Copeman, (1) in Col. Cox's (2) Regiment, & he thinks the Colonel's Christian name was Ebenezer—that deponent resided at that time in the then town of Canajoharie in the County of Tryon, now Danube Herkimer County—and once Minden Montgomery County—

That the first time they were called out they went to Caughnawaga, that Genl Herkimer had the command, Col. Cox was then with his Regiment, and there was a report when they went out that there would be a battle, but when they got there they did not fight, the regiment was paraded several times on the ice of the Mohawk River, and they remained there three or four days, and then they marched up to Johnstown about a mile above the village they were there about a day he thinks & then they marched down to Caughnawaga where they staid about a day & then they went home—that it was said that a treaty had been made with Sir John Johnson (4) that he should not take up arms against the county—thinks they were absent from home ten or twelve days—thinks it was about twenty four or five miles that they went from home—

That in the spring of the same year & he thinks in May there was a report that the Indians & Tories were collecting in Johnstown the company was called out to go down there, that the company came up with the rest of the regiment or rather the regiment assembled first before the Nose so called on the Mohawk Rivers at a tavern which was kept close by that he thinks his name was McKinsey—then the regiment under the command of Col. Cox marched down to Caughnawaga again, where they remained a day or two thinks two days & then they returned home again, did not find any Indians or Tories, the Regiment he thinks was dismissed at Kursey's Tavern near the Nose as above mentioned, that he thinks he was out this time a week—that in a short time after they came back it was reported that Guy Johnson (5) & one Col. Clause (6) who lived below Johnstown & down by Tripes Hill, was coming up the Mohawk with flour, rum & other liquors brandy, gin etc. and it was said that the flour barrels had keggs of powder inside of the flour—when Capt. Copeman's company & Capt. Crouse's (7) Company were called out to march up and follow the boats up the Mohawk River, and when they came up to Fort Herkimer they met the Herkimer, people under Col. Bellinger thinks his name was Peter Bellinger (8) & Major Clapsattle was there.

Bellinger took command of the detachment and then marched up to Fort Stanwix and found the boats there, the boats were mostly unloaded and the barrels were carried across to Wood Creek about two miles, they went to this place & found them lying on the banks of the creek & Capt. Copeman was the man who inspected the boats& the barrels, bore holes in the flour Bbls & tiped the liquor barrels & threw some liquor out—that Maj. Clapsattle told Capt. Copeman that he did not inspect them sufficiently, Copeman said if he did not like it, he might inspect them himself, Clapsattle said he would make him do it—Copemen jumped out of the boat where he then was & told Clapsattle to come on & make him do it, & drew his sword--and afterwards stuck his sword in the ground & said he would try him with his hands—the men were stationed around the barrells & kept guard—they found no powder but some excellent liquor—and they remained there three or four days, and then they marched home. That deponent thinks they were absent about ten or twelve days—thinks this was in the month of June—and in about a week or two there was an order come from Genl. Schuyler that each company in the Regiment should furnish ten men as a guard to the Genl. Who was going up to the German Flatts to make a treaty with the Five Nations of Indians, deponent was one of the ten, the company was called out & they drew lots—and they came up to Fort Herkimer, Capt. Brown (9) who came from Durlock (10) with some men here took command and marched them over to the present Village of Herkimer, where there was some houses but no fort.

The object of Genl. Schuyler was to make a treaty with the Indians, there were a great many Indians with him at that time—Staid at Herkimer nearly a fortnight before the Indians all got together, & in this time the men were employed in cutting pickets to make a fort, (11) made a beginning at the work & was then discharged—then went home again, was absent this time about three weeks—He remained at home some time but can not say exactly how long, it was reported that the Indians were collecting again, that deponent was again called out & he and Capt. Copeman and the whole company & deponent thinks Capt. Dievendorff's (12) company was also along, they came up through the woods to the Indian Castle about eight or ten miles, that they lay out in the woods the first night near the castle, staid there a day or two, kept guard part of them & some went into the woods further to see if they could find any Indians—that he was out this time about four days—This deponent was also out on scouting parties several times, but he can not say how often during this fall—that this deponent thinks he performed duty during the year as much as three months, although he can not recollect the exact time he was out on each occasion.—

And this deponent further says that in the year 1777—according to his best recollection the Militia was called out again, but cannot recollect the months, thinks it must have been the last of April or first of May—that part of the company only was called out under the command of Lieut. George Raisnor (13)—

deponent can not recollect who was the Capt. was – that there was a draft from each company in the Regiment of men & officers, but he can not recollect that there was any field officer along— thinks there was somewhat more than a hundred men out at this time—they marched back of Johnstown to a place called Sakindaga—to see if there were any Indians & Tories collected there, but did not find any, can not say exactly how long they were there, remained at Johnstown a while when they were out & when they came back—the orders were to take three days provisions with them, but after they were at Johnstown they drew provisions—were out about two weeks & then marched back to Fort Plain & were then dismissed. That he was sent out as a scout after this up the Geisibergh or Goat Hill as it is translated— when the company had a rendezvous & then Capt. Copeman used to send them from here, sometimes only two or three men were sent, sometimes ten or a dozen & frequently more—and their turns would come often to go, they were out sometimes two days & sometimes only one—after this time & he thinks in May there was a report that the Indians were coming back upon the German Flatts the whole regiment was then called out & they mustered at Little Fall Hill where one Dygert, Capt. Peter Dygert (14) kept a Tavern—there the Regiment marched up to Fort Herkimer there was a fort & a block house there—when they learned it was a false alarm, it was reported that the Indians had said they would burn off the flatts—remained at the fort two or three days, and then went back as far as Dygert's Tavern & were dismissed—and after they returned home they were employed as scouts and sometime on guard, it was considered a dangerous time, and on every report whether true or false the men were assembled—and went out sometimes a day & sometimes only a night—

And this deponent further says, that in the latter part of June or in the early part of July in that year 1777—he was called out again together with a part of the company that Capt. Crouse of the same Regiment had command of this deponent and part of his company was out don't recollect any of his company officers were along—that the Regiment assembled at Cherry Valley where there a settlement—Genl Herkimer then had the command, they were at Cherry Valley a day or more can not say how long, then marched down to Otsego Lake to the mouth or out let of the lake, a few houses only there, now called Cooperstown, then only about ten acres of land cleared—then Marched down towards the Unadilla River there was a foot path through the woods, something of a road along the river—when they got there they came to a halt, & some one was sent for the Indians to meet them (as he understood) at the Oquago—Brant was then with from two to three hundred Indians Genl. Herkimer & Col. Cox after they had fixed upon a time met Brant & they had a talk –neither party was allowed to bring guns to the place where they were talking, there was a place covered for them to talk under & a place for a table—there was men stationed out to keep guard & the Indians had seats made of boards under the trees that they sat on, but without arms—Gen. Herkimer & Col. Brandt (15) talked a while then Col. Cox spoke & said damn him & let him go—Brandt mentioned this in Indian to his men who were close by—they all at once sprang up & shouted, patting their hands on their mouths as they hollered and then ran off—and directly they heard them firing their pieces—Genl Herkimer took Brant by the arm & told him not to mind what Cox said, that they were old neighbors & ought not to be spilling each other's blood &c. Herkimer talked very nice to him – Brant was moderate too.

The day before this public meeting Genl. Herkimer & Brandt had talked a good deal together about the business— understood there was a treaty made & that Brandt would come back & live on the River again—they returned the same way as far as Otego, then Col. Bellinger's Regiment went home by a place called the Butternuts as he understood—and deponent's Regt commanded by Col. Cox went home by the way of Otsego lake & Cherry Valley & that they were gone in all the time about seventeen or eighteen days – When they again done duty on guard as before & on scouts wherever required, which was pretty often—

That the next call was that they should go to Herkimer, this was in August according to his best recollection & in the year 1777, the same year that they went to Unadilla—the whole regiment was called out, & they marched up to Herkimer, and stopped at Fort Dayton, it was said that Genl. Arnold (16) was coming up the River with some troops & Genl Herkimer kept them here some days to get his men together & writing for Arnold to come up—

But they marched out before Genl. Arnold came, as the committee would not wait any longer—first day they went—little above the German settlement eight or ten miles from Fort Dayton where they remained all night—next day went as far as Oriskany were [where] they slept one night & Genl Herkimer then wanted to stay until Arnold came up—they however started in the morning to go to Fort Stanwix (17) and had not gone far, as early as eight or nine in the morning the battle began with the Indians— Deponent's company was he thinks was about in the center of the detachment—they stood their ground a little while about half an hour when he lost sight of most of his officers saw one of them going back & then he did, one Christopher Eckler (18)he recollects was close by him & they retreated together until they got out of the swamp, then they ran pretty fast, until they got over the river on the north side—and they then came to Fort Dayton where they remained about one day & then they went home. Deponent was engaged inquiring for his brother (19) & could hear nothing of him & went home to see if he was there—but learned afterwards that he had been killed in the battle that Col. Cox was also killed in the battle & Lieut. Resnor of his company.

Deponent was home but a day or two when he was called out again & it was said Genl. Arnold had arrived at Fort Dayton & they marched back up the river again as far as Dygert's Tavern at

Little Fall Hill where the Regiment was to meet again—and here they learned that the enemy had all gone back and left Fort Stanwix -and they were dismissed again—that they were out in all this time as much as two weeks. That the remainder of this summer deponent was on duty from time to time as above mentioned in keeping guard and in various scouts about the country—and he thinks he done duty that year in all about four months, as it was as late as Christmas before they were discharged.

And this deponent further says that during the fall of this same year 1777, and he thinks in September or October he marched under one Capt. Seeber (20) who was adjutant of the Regiment; that part of the company only was called out; that the militia was to assemble at Schenectady—that the object was to reinforce the American Army at Saratoga or Stillwater—that deponent became sick with the dissentary before he got to Schenectady & was left behind & in a day or two returned home that he heard that the militia did not get to Stillwater (21) until after the battle was over—that he was absent about a week at this time.

And this deponent further says, that in the early part of the year 1778, he was employed most of the time in doing duty in the forts & going on scouting parties as he was required by his officers, being still under the command of Capt. Copeman—that in May as near as he can now recollect, he was called upon to go to Cherry Valley with his company, that Copeman was with the company, there was Capt. Lipe's (22) Company being the same company formerly commanded by Capt. Crouse who was killed at Oriskany--& another company commanded by Capt. Jacob Dievendorff (23) that Henry Dievendorff the former Capt. was also killed at Oriskany & Jacob the Lieut. was made Capt. then these companies he recollects of were together at that time Col. Clyde (24) had command of the detachment—arrived at Cherry Valley the first day, staid there one night & then next day, sent out a party scouting while they were there—then went to Springfield & there staid one night & then marched home again, thinks on this expedition they must have been absent five or six days before they got home.

That after this he was called out to stand guard at Fort Walradt. That there was no officer there higher than an Ensign & the one in this fort was named Henry Walradt, then they first employed in building the fort and spent all most the whole of the summer in that fort doing duty as a guard and once in a while on a scouting party—that he was obliged to do duty either at Fort Walradt or at Fort Plank—that Col. Clyde had command of all these forts in the beat of this regiment, Capt. Copeman was at fort Plank most of the time, his family lived about two miles from them—when he was not at the fort, & Lieut. House had the command—that he done duty until the snow fell in the fall—

That sometime in this year but he can not say exactly when, he was out at Cherry Valley again with a part of the company, Capt. Seeber (26) was along, one Peter Wormouth (27) was killed by the Indians, & Peter Sitts was taken prisoner, these were on express from Fort Plain to the Village of Cherry Valley (28)—thinks it was in the summer, it was before the burning of Cherry Valley—In the same year also deponent was at Herkimer under Capt. Brown who was from Durlock—that they were either on scouts or on guard on the fort, at Fort Dayton—thinks he was there about two weeks or perhaps three—when he returned he went to Fort Plank—that while he was on Scouts this year he recollects of going out to the Salt Spring three times, went over the Squago [Otsquago] Creek two or three times, in the course of that summer & fall--& thinks he was out more than four months on duty—

And this deponent further says, that in the year 1779, he was also employed in doing duty in these forts as in the preceding year, that he was still in the same company commanded as aforesaid—that the first time they were out that year that he can now recollect the Col. Call out the whole regiment to go to Fort Herkimer, a distance of about twenty eight miles—and remained at that place about two or three weeks, that the principal duty was keeping guard and going out on scouts once in a while—then wait [sic went] back to Fort Walradt.

That the same year they were called out to Palatine, this was in the latter part of the summer & only part of the company went out—& was gone about a week before they got back—that in haying time of that year four Indians made a prisoner of one Orren Davy; (29) who was carried off by them, twenty or thirty men & of whom this deponent was one, went in pursuit, & over took the Indians & found that Davy was killed, they did not kill any Indians or make any prisoners—it was said that Brandt was among them, & that he was wounded in the foot.

That in the month of September & October they were marched up again to Herkimer, Fort Dayton, under command of Capt. Brown they staid in the fort & that time about two weeks—this was the second time he was at Fort Dayton under this Capt. Brown that part of the company only was out—that at the end of two weeks they expected to be relieved, but were not--& had to go to Fort Stanwix to guard some boats under command of Capt. Brown, went to Fort Stanwix & remained there until the boats were unloaded & the boats brought back some hides, that before he returned he was gone about four weeks, that it was cold icy weather when they returned home late in the fall—that he thinks this year he done duty about five months & that he was actually employed & under arms that length of time.

And this deponent further says that in the year 1780 he was again under the same officers doing about the same kind of duty, etc., on guard as a soldier in the fort or on some Indian trail as a spy or scout as in the former years, that he was in Fort Plank part of the time & part of the time in Fort Clyde & some times in Fort Bary (30)—that in the month of July or early in August was marched from Fort Plank to Fort Herkimer and up to Fort

Stanwix, that the Col. was out with the whole Regiment, Col. Waggoner's (31) Regiment was also out & he believes Col. Bellinger's Regiment—that Genl. Van Rensselaer (32) was in command of these troops—Deponent did not see him until they come at Herkimer—

They all marched up to Fort Stanwix where they remained until the boats were unloaded, that there was a great many goods come up the river on boats when Van Rensselaer came up—that when he arrived at the Fort they were saluted from the fort by a great many guns, & the whole line cheered—Col. Clyde commanded the Regt & Peter Dygert was a Major at that time—**that he was gone on this occasion about twelve or fourteen days when they got back to Herkimer they heard that the Indians were burning off the county below in the neighborhood of Fort Plain & Fort Plank, destroying the whole settlement, killed a great many and took many women & children prisoners.**

That each man hurried back as fast as he could without reference to any orders, each one anxious to see what had become of his family and friends—Fort Walradt was burned & deponent's clothes were burned & his horses killed by the enemy, that his brother in law kept these horses by the fort and worked a farm about a quarter of a mile off—that deponent was then put in Fort Plank where he done duty the rest of the season except when he was out on scouting parties. That in the fall of the same year, Sir John Johnson came up the North side of the Mohawk River with a large body of Indians and Tories and destroyed the greater part of the country, that the whole militia of the county were called out under Genl. Van Rensselaer (33) except those who were left to guard the forts and old men unable to do duty—that deponent was left at home to do duty in the Fort where he then was, and continued to do duty until late in the fall of that year—except when he was out on scouts—that he thinks in this year he done duty more than four months.—

That he recollects that one Nellis (34) was killed by the Indians in this year, & his father wounded in the arm close by Fort Windecker, that deponent & others were called out in pursuit & after they returned deponent was stationed at Fort Windecker a week—that is in the course of the week or so, there were two men killed by the Indians, Woolver & Casler (35) and Deponent was again called out as a scout in pursuit of the Indians—That it was dangerous for a person to be out of the forts as the Indians were always on the look out and skulking about—

And this deponent further says that a man by the name of John Ecker Enlisted in Capt. Putman's (36) Company in Col. Willett's Regiment of "Nine Months Men" so called that the man got tired and was very anxious to get a substitute—and deponent enlisted in his place as a substitute that was in the month of June. He served in this company until the month of December when he was dismissed about Christmas, at Fort Plank in the County of Tryon aforesaid—that he did not receive any discharge—

That the first service since he done after his enlistment was service in the Fort, standing guard, & doing substantially the same duty that he done in the militia service in the preceding years—that he was sometimes in one of these forts & sometimes in another—that in this year he was out at a place called Turlock under the Col. of the Regiment Marinus Willett, it was said that the Tories & Indians had been plundering cattle, horses, sheep etc. and they were collected in that place—that the first time they went out there was some 25 men, they could not find the cattle & after remaining one night they returned again to Fort Plank—they got back in; the afternoon & before night they had orders to assemble at Fort Plain where the whole Regiment got together, and a number of militia who volunteered, they started that night in the dark, and proceeded to Fort Clyde, then to Bowman's Creek, that when they got to Turlock it was day light, that the men were put in order in two lines, that some men were set forward & Lieut. Sammons (37) with them to draw out the enemy, which they succeeded in doing, (then retreated and led them in between these two lines of men who fired upon them with great effect—the Indians retreated and Col. Willett & his men kept the ground—that they tried to find the Indians but could not & then retreated or marched back again one Capt. McKean (38) was wounded, the soldiers brought him out & he afterwards died of his wounds—one Bellinger (39) was also killed, Casper Near (40) was also killed then some wounded.—

That they were out about two days and one night and remained in the Forts on duty as before and going on Scouts, until in the fall of the year, & he thinks in the month of October when Major Ross (41) & Walter Butler were said to be at Johnstown, then the Col. ordered his regiment out again & the militia all turned out again to meet the enemy, when they got there the enemy was prepared for battle & an engagement took place which commenced in the woods, our men then retreated in the open fields, the new levies retreated until the militia came up when they rallied—the Americans lost a field piece then retook it—and at length the enemy gave way again, when the field piece was taken Col. Willett laid his hand on it and said, "Hurra for Lady Washington"--was a brass 6 (42) & the enemy retreated into the country towards the head of the Canada Creek on the hills above the river—the troops under Col. Willet came up the river, Maj. Copeman was also along with his militia, he behaved well at Johnstown—the Americans came up as far as Herkimer then went up the Canada Creek, and staid in the woods one night, and then followed on again until they came up with them at the place where two rods [roads] came together, here there was some firing, one Artillery (43) man on the American side was killed, & some prisoners were taken from the enemy—Deponent was not present when Butler (44) was killed—when he came up a man on the other side of the river was holding up his commission & waiving [waving]- said he had Butler's commission.

That after this they all returned home, going back by the way of Remeysnyder's Bush & Snell's Bush—they had some prisoners with them—they were two days without any provisions, the inhabitants then met them & sent them some provisions—they took the prisoners to Fort Plain & then delivered them to Col. Willet who sent them below—that he done duty until the month of December & about Christmas—that he done one month's duty before he returned into Willett's Regiment & did duty in that Regiment about six months or more—

And this deponent further says that in the next year which was 1782 he continued to do duty as before in the Militia company under Capt. House (45) doing duty in the Forts & going out on scouts from time to time—during all that summer, & in the winter they were not obliged to mount guard, that this year they were not much troubled with the Indians or Tories—and that he did not do over three months duty in that year.

And this deponent further says that in the next year 1783 he did not do any service at all, the war having been considered as ended.

That this deponent was engaged in the battle of Oriskany, Johnstown & Durlock—that he never had any written discharge.
And to the several questions put by the court this deponent says—

That he was born in the Town of Canajoharie, in the year 1757.

That he has a record of his age kept by his father in a large Dutch Bible with brass clasps now in his possession—

That he resided at the commencement of his services at Canajoharie in the then County of Tryon, and has resided since the war a few years in the same town, then moved five or six miles which by the division of towns & Counties has made him now in the town of Danube in the County of Herkimer where he at present resided.—

That he was in the militia & ordered out, sometimes volunteered & once a substitute for one John Ecker—that he done duty & was acquainted with Marinus Willett—has seen Col. Gansvoort (46) --& Col. Renier (47) who was one winter at Fort Plank.

That he never received a discharge from the service.

That he is acquainted with no clergyman who can testify to his character & that John Roth & Richard Shimel of Stark can prove the service and can testify to his character & that he thinks

he can prove his service by Jacob A. Young or part of them.

He hereby relinquishes every claim whatever to a pension or annuity except the present, and he declares that his name is not on the pension roll of any agency in any state. (Signed with his mark) John Dusler

Sworn to & subscribed the day & year aforesaid in open court. Julius C. Nelson, Clerk

End Notes—W.16244—John Duesler

1. Abraham Copeman was appointed Captain on August 26, 1775 of the Sixth Company in Colonel Nicholas Herkimer's First Regiment of Tryon County Militia. So far muster rolls for this company have not been found.

2. On September 5, 1776, Colonel Herkimer was appointed Brigadier General of the Tryon County Militia Brigade. Lieutenant-Colonel Ebenezer Cox of Herkimer's Regiment was appointed Colonel in his place and Major William Seeber was appointed Lieutenant-Colonel in place of Cox.

3. This happened in January of 1776. Herkimer at this time was still a colonel. It was Major General Philip Schuyler who had marched from Albany with a large number of Albany County Militia and joined forces with the Tryon County Militia at Caughnawaga.

4. Sir John Johnson son of the late Sir William Johnson now living at Johnson Hall in Johnstown was one of the active and influential loyalists against the American cause.

5. Guy Johnson, Nephew and son-in-law of Sir William Johnson another active and influential loyalist. Guy Johnson had been Colonel of the Third Regiment of Tryon County Militia until Frederick Visscher was elected and then appointed Colonel of the regiment on August 26, 1775.

6. Colonel Daniel Claus, also a son-in-law of the late Sir William Johnson. He also had been Colonel of one of the Tryon County Militia Regiments until August 26, 1775 when he was replaced. His home near the present day Amsterdam, New York burned in May of 1780.

7. Robert Crouse was appointed captain in April of 1776 of the Fourth Company in Colonel Cox's Regiment. Captain Jacob W. Seeber the original Captain of the Fourth Company had accepted a captain's commission in Colonel Cornelius D. Wynkoop's Fourth New York Continental Regiment.

8. Colonel Peter Bellinger and Major Augustinus Clapsattle of the Fourth Regiment of Tryon County Militia.

9. John Mathias Brown was the Captain of the Eighth Company in Colonel Cox's Regiment.

10. New Dorlach now present day Sharon Springs, Schoharie County, New York.

11. The fort was being built by various troops but it was under the supervision Colonel Elias Dayton of the Third New Jersey Continental Regiment. The fort was completed in August of 1776 and was named Fort Dayton after Colonel Dayton.

12. Henry Dieffendorf was appointed Captain of the Fifth Company on August 26, 1775 in Colonel Herkimer's later Cox's Regiment.

13. George Resner, (Rasnier, etc.) was the first lieutenant in Captain Copeman's Company. He was commissioned on June 25, 1778 but he had been killed at the Battle of Oriskany on August 6, 1777.

14. Peter S. Dygert was appointed Captain of the Third Company on August 26, 1775 in Colonel Herkimer's and later Cox's Regiment. Dygert was later appointed major and he was commissioned on March 4, 1780.

15. Joseph Brant was a captain not a colonel. This meeting took place on June 27, 1777 at Unadilla.

16. Major General Benedict Arnold. General Herkimer had asked for reinforcements from Albany. General Arnold was with the main army on the Hudson River near Stillwater which was being pursued by the forces under the command of Lieutenant General John Burgoyne.

17. Fort Schuyler in the present day City of Rome, Oneida County, New York, was besieged by another British force under Brigadier General Barry St. Leger. General Herkimer with the Tryon County Militia Brigade was marching to the assistance of the garrison in Fort Schuyler. The Battle of Oriskany was fought on August 6, 1777.

18. Christopher Eckler in his pension application R.3239 makes no mention of his being at the Battle of Oriskany. Christopher served in Captain Henry Eckler's Company; this was his brother, in Colonel Bellinger's Regiment. Later the Eckler's removed from the Kyle (Chyle) Settlement and moved to the area near Fort Plank. They then served in Captain Copeman's Company.

19. So far I haven't found John's brother's Christian name. The brothers that are known are Marcus and Jacob.

20. Captain Jacob W. Seeber had been killed at Oriskany. Also Ensign Adolph Seeber, and Lieutenant Severinus Seeber had been killed at Oriskany. Lieutenant-Colonel William Seeber was badly wounded and died of his wounds on September 1, 1777. A Jacob Seeber was commissioned Adjutant on October 19, 1779 in place of James Cannon who had been commissioned Adjutant on June 25, 1778. Samuel Clyde was appointed adjutant on August 26, 1775.

21. Several detachments of the Tryon County Militia had been at Stillwater since late August and early September. They were being used as teamsters and to build fortifications. A detachment of the Tryon County Militia was in the October 7, 1777 battle under General Arnold. There was no other way to get to Stillwater in large numbers and with provisions and other supplies except by water from Albany. Dysentery was a common camp disorder as was small pox.

22. Actually in 1778, Francis Utt or Ult was captain of the former Crouse's Company. Utt had served as first lieutenant and Adam Leipe as second lieutenant under Crouse. In 1779, Utt had removed from the area and Leipe was then appointed Captain. He was commissioned on March 4, 1780.

23. Jacob Dieffendorf had served as the first lieutenant in his brother Henry's Company. Jacob was commissioned as captain on March 4, 1780.

24. After the deaths of Colonel Cox and Lieutenant-Colonel Seeber, Samuel Campbell and Samuel Clyde were appointed Colonel and Lieutenant-Colonel respectively. They were commissioned on June 25, 1778.

25. Henry Walrath was commissioned ensign on March 4, 1780 in Captain Jost or Joseph House's Company. Captain Copeman had been promoted to major and he was commissioned on October 19, 1779. This was the home of Ensign Walrath which was burnt on August 2, 1780 by Captain Brant and his forces.

26. Duesler again is referring to Adjutant and Lieutenant Jacob Seeber.

27. It was Matthew Wormuth who was a second lieutenant and Peter Sitts who was an ensign in Captain John Hess' Company in Colonel Jacob Klock's Second Regiment of Tryon County Militia. Wormuth and Sitts were surprised by Captain Brant on June 2, 1778 near Cherry Valley. Wormuth tried to escape and he was killed. Ensign Sitts was kept a prisoner until he was released on June 9, 1780.

28. Cherry Valley was destroyed on November 11, 1778 by forces under Captain Walter Butler and Joseph Brant.

29. Probably Aaron or Arendt Davy who was a private in Captain Dieffendorf's Company.

30. First time a Fort Bary has been referred to.

31. Peter Wagner, Sr., or Waggoner, etc. was the Lieutenant-Colonel of Colonel Klock's Regiment. His home still stands today and Route 5 above Nelliston, New York but it is privately owned.

32. Robert VanRensselaer was appointed brigadier general on June 16, 1780. The Tryon County Militia was part of this brigade. This incident happened during the last part of July and first part of August in 1780. Brant and Cornplanter destroyed what is now the town of Minden and Village of Fort Plain area, Montgomery County, NY on August 2, 1780.

33. This was in October of 1780. Sir John Johnson invaded the Schoharie Valley on October 17, 1780. He

reached Stone Arabia on October 19th about mid-morning and attacked an American force of Massachusetts Levies and Tryon county Militia under Colonel John Brown. Colonel Brown was killed and about forty of his men were killed Major Oliver Root retreated with the remainder back to Fort Paris. Johnson after destroying Stone Arabia but unable to capture Fort Paris or Fort Keyser continued his march toward Oneida Lake. Late in the afternoon General VanRensselaer with Albany County Militia, New York Levies and Tryon County Militia caught up with Johnson near the present day Village of St. Johnsville, Montgomery County, New York and a second battle was fought on that day. Johnson was able to escape under the cover of darkness back to Fort Oswego.

34. A Jacob Nellis was killed on June 27, 1780. This might be the Nellis he is referring to.

35. This actually happened on July 18, 1781. Brothers John, Nicholas, and Peter Wollever and their brother-in-law Peter Casler were driving cattle to Fort Rensselaer when they were attacked. Casler and Nicholas Wollever were killed.

36. John served as a private in Captain Garret Putman's Company in Lieutenant-Colonel Commandant Marinus Willett's Regiment of New York State Levies in 1781. On a pay receipt roll dated for 1785 John Tussler was owed £9..8..5 for his service in Willett's but it appears he never received it. There is no signature opposite his name and the column for his money is not in the same column as those that had a signature opposite their names. FROM: Revolutionary War Rolls 1775-1783, Series M-246, Roll 78, folder 173, National Archives, Washington, D.C.

37. Lieutenant Jacob Sammons of Captain Lawrence Gross' Company of Willett's Regiment. Lieutenant Sammons with ten men was sent to attack the Indians who were fixing breakfast etc. The ruse worked as they pursued Sammons and party into Willett's well planned ambush.

38. Captain Robert McKean of Willett's Regiment and his son Samuel, of Captain Elihu Marshall's Company of Willett's Regiment was also wounded. The Battle of New Dorlach was fought on July 10, 1781.

39. Frederick Bellinger of the Tryon County Militia and Adam Kittle of Capt. Gross's Company were part of Lieutenant Sammon's detachment. They were so closely pursued by the Indians that as they reached Willett's prepared ambush site, Willett's men fired prematurely into the pursuing Indians to prevent the whole party from being overtaken but Bellinger and Kittle were killed before they made the American forces line.

40. Casper Nier or Neahr, Near, etc., of Captain Gross' Company was also killed during the ensuing battle.

41. On October 24, 1781, Major John Ross of the King's Royal Regiment of New York which was Sir John Johnsons' Regiment, they were never called Johnson's Green's until the 19th century writers started writing about the American Revolution in the Mohawk Valley, and Captain Walter Butler of Butler's Rangers which was raised by his father Lieutenant-Colonel John Butler, and Captain Gilbert Tice of the Indian Department (Tice was formerly a tavern owner in Johnstown) burnt Warren's Bush, (now the Town of Florida, Montgomery County, N.Y.) and the surrounding areas and marched to the Village of Johnstown on October 25th to rest, collect intelligence

and food for their return march to Fort Oswego. Late in the afternoon Willett with a mixed force of Massachusetts and New York Levies, Tryon County Militia and Captain Andrew Moody and his company of the Second Continental Artillery Regiment arrived in Johnstown and attacked Ross's forces. After hours of fighting Major Ross escaped under cover of darkness.

42. Captain Moody actually had only a brass 3 pounder. This means it shot a solid cannonball that weighed 3 pounds.

43. The artillery man that was killed was Jesse Wood of Moody's Company.

44. Captain Butler was killed in the skirmish at West Canada Creek on October 30, 1781.

45. According to "A Recipt of Capt Joseph House", dated "Canajohary District September 24th 1784", John Dusler had two certificates, No. 11041 for £4..15..— and 10934 for £1..10..1. it was signed with his mark. FROM: Revolutionary War Rolls 1775-1783, Series M-246, Roll 72, folder 89, National Archives, Washington, D.C.

46. Peter Gansevoort was the Colonel of the Third New York Continental Regiment.

47. Pierre Regnier was the Lieutenant-Colonel of the Fourth New York Continental Regiment.

Pension Application for William Feeter or Vetter

(Transcribed by Wayne Lenig)

S.13013

Declaration in order to obtain the benefit of the Act of Congress passed June 7, 1832

State of New York

Herkimer County

On this 11h day of [October personally – crossed out] February in the year 1833 personally appeared in open court, before the Judges of the Court of Common Pleas, now sitting, William Feeter, a resident of the Town of Little Falls in the County of Herkimer & State of New York aged seventy-six years, who being first duly sworn according to law, doth on his oath, make the following declaration, in order to obtain the benefit of the Act of Congress passed June 7, 1832.

That he entered the service of the United States under the following named officers, & served as herein stated.

That deponent was born at the place called Stone Arabia in the (now) Town of Palatine in the County of Montgomery & State of New York, the second day of February in the year 1756. Deponent has been informed, there was a record of his age made by the clergyman of the Dutch Reformed Church at Stone Arabia, but deponent never saw it, & does not know where said record is. Deponent's father also had a record of the ages of his children which has been destroyed, & these are the only records of his age of which he has any knowledge that at the time deponent entered into the service he lived at the (now) town of Amsterdam in said County of Montgomery in said State of New York with his father, & since the Revolutionary War, deponent has resided in the said Town of Little Falls, where he still resides.

Deponent was enrolled in a company of militia at Amsterdam aforesaid in a company Commanded by [David – crossed out] Emmanuel Degraff Capt. The other officers of the company deponent does not now recollect, in the spring of the year 1776. During this year deponent was out several times with his company on scouting parties, & went to Johnstown, Caughnawaga & Sockandaga - all now in the said County of Montgomery. Deponent was out several days each time, in pursuit of Indians & Tories who infested the county. Deponent does not recollect of being out in service at any time during the succeeding winter.

The spring following - the year 1777, deponent was out several time on scouting parties in pursuit of Indians & Tories. The last of June or first of July deponent was drafted to go with the militia to Fort Stanwix to shut up Wood Creek that empties into Oneida Lake, Deponent went in a company commanded by Abraham Yates Captain. The other officers deponent does not now recollect. The company went to Fort Stanwix from which place a guard was sent to protect the militia while they fell trees into the creek to prevent the British from assending it with boats. Deponent does not recollect how long they were engaged there, but when they returned to Amsterdam deponent thinks the militia had been out three or four weeks. That at the time deponent returned from Fort Stanwix as above stated, the county was all in commotion, it was known that St. Leger was on his way from Oswego to attack Fort Stanwix, Burgoyne was advancing from the north & Howe triumphant at New York, the Tories held up their heads & were confident, their cause would succeed. Most of the inhabitants at Amsterdam were Tories, as were the father & brothers of deponent - who a few days after the Battle at Oriskany, which was on the 6th of August - turned deponent out of doors because he was a friend to his county, & deponent went immediately to Stone Arabia where he was born, & where most of the inhabitants were Whigs. Deponent went to the house of his uncle, George Steers, who in a few days went with deponent to a family of Grays, & they gave deponent a musket & the necessary equippage. Deponent was then enrolled in a Company of Militia Commanded by Sufrinus Cook Capt, Nicholas Coppernol Lieutenant, & Peter Greimes [Gremps] Junior Ensign.

This was soon after the Battle at Oriskany, & the Indians & Tories infested the county & deponent with this company was almost constantly engaged in pursuit of them. Stone Arabia is a high range of land from which could be seen the surrounding country for a great many miles, & the militia were told that where a large smoke was seen to rise in any part of the county, [they were ordered – crossed out] to turn out immediately, & deponent was out several times this summer in pursuit of the enemy from this same sign. The company to which deponent belonged was attached to a regiment commanded by Jacob Klock Col & Peter Waggoner was Lieutenant Col, the other officers deponent does not now recollect. The next spring deponent was drafted to go to Unadilla, the Indians & Tories as it was reported had collected therein. Deponent went in a company Commanded by Samuel Gray, Captain, the other officers deponent does not now recollect. The militia rendyvoused at Fort Herkimer. The day before deponent went to Fort Herkimer an Indian spy was taken prisoner in the Mohawk River & was bro[ugh]t to the fort. The same day deponent arrived at Fort Herkimer, he & one Jacob Sant was sent with the Indian spy to Jacob Klock's, the Colonel of the Regiment at Stone Arabia, who was directed to send the Indian to Albany. Deponent & said Sant returned immediately to Fort Herkimer. A few days after a party of Indians & Tories amounting to eight or nine hundred made their appearance in the vicinity of the fort. The Indian spy above mentioned was, as was supposed, sent out by this party to scout the country & gain intelligence. The inhabitants had information of the approach of the enemy & had moved into Fort Herkimer & Dayton. A scouting party had been sent from the fort down the Unadilla River to assertain the situation & strength of the enemy. This party was attacked by the Indians & most of them killed. One or two returned to the fort & informed the inhabitants of the approach of the enemy. About all the buildings & property were burnt & destroyed along the Mohawk River by the enemy in the vicinity of the forts. A party of Indians kept at a short distance from Fort Herkimer which contained only about 100 militia. The Indians set a house on fire a short distance from the fort. Deponent & several others climbed over the pickets of the fort & ran & put the fire out & saved the house. The enemy stayed but one day in the neighborhood. The militia did not go to Unadilla. Deponent remained at Fort Herkimer some time, cannot tell how long. The militia were ordered to go from Fort Herkimer to Glaisburgh [Klauberg] in the (now) Town of Minden in the County of Montgomery about two miles west of Fort Plain. The militia at that place were under the command of Colonel Jacob Klock. They lay at the latter place till the massacre & destruction of Cherry Valley in the now County of Otsego, that joins Montgomery County on the southwest. The first of November the news spread through the country, & the militia at Glaisburgh went in pursuit of the enemy. They arrived within a few miles of Cherry Valley & encamped at a small house for the night; Deponent & one George Waffle were sent to scout the woods in the vicinity of the house when they encamped to assertain if the enemy were in the vicinity. The next morning the militia marched to Cherry Valley & the garrison were collecting the dead into the fort. The militia under the command of Col. Jacob Klock returned to the (now) Town of Minden near Fort Plain & lay at the house of one Mr. Seeber. Deponent thinks soon after this he returned to Stone Arabia. The last of November or the first of December the Indians made their appearance in the north part of Stone Arabia. The militia were called out & deponent went with them to scout the county in pursuit of the Indians & were out a day or two. A few days after this the Indians again appeared in the same part of Stone Arabia & took a few prisoners & deponent & the militia went again in pursuit.

The next March in the year 1779, the Indians & Tories, as it was reported had collected in the north part of Stone Arabia in a settlement called Tilloborough. The militia were called out & deponent went in a company commanded by Samuel Gray. The militia collected at the house of Capt. Christian Getman, which was picketed & where at times regular troops lay, & where a guard was kept. The militia was out a few days. Deponent & one Peter Getman were sent out to scout the country, went on show shoes could find no Indians & returned to Stone Arabia. In February preceding a company was enlisted at Stone Arabia under Capt. Samuel Gray for the purpose of carrying provisions & ammunition from Schenectady to Fort Stanwix in boats, & to the other forts between, located near the Mohawk River. The company mustered at Albany in February & was then sent home till the river opened in the spring. In April as deponent believes, the company again mustered at Albany, & then went to Schenectady to load the boats & proceed up the river to Fort Stanwix. Colonel VanSchaick commanded a regiment of troops that went in company with the boats; from Fort Stanwix Col VanSchaick Regiment & Captain Grays Company went to Fort Bruewington [Brewerton] at the outlet of Oneida Lake, where this Captain Grays Company & a small guard remained, & the regiment proceeded to destroy Oneida Castle. (1) The troops returned in a few days & brot with them about thirty Indians prisoners, who were put on board the boat & taken to Schenectady. The boatmen, being Capt. Gray's company, went twice after this to Fort Stanwix, as deponent believes. In June deponent thinks, the boatmen had permission to volunteer & go with the troops under the Command of General Clinton, who had passed up the Mohawk River early in the Spring to Canajoharie & from there had proceeded to Cooperstown at the foot of Otsego Lake, in the now County of Otsego. Deponent with several others of the boatmen joined the troops & Genl. Clinton at Cooperstown. They remained there a few weeks & then Genl. Clinton proceeded down the river & joined Genl. Sullivan at Tioga about the middle of August as deponent believes. The army under the Command of Genl. Sullivan marched soon after to Chemung about twelves miles as deponent believes. The next day the army met the whole force of the Indians & Tories at Newtown. A battle was fought the enemy was soon driven from the position & retreated. Deponent was solicited to help man boats to convey the wounded to Tioga & from there to

Wyoming about one hundred miles below Tioga on the Susquehannah River. From the latter place deponent returned with the boats to carry provisions to the fort at Tioga, at which deponent remained till Genl. Sullivan returned from his expedition in the Indian County. Deponent went with the army to Wyoming & from there to Easton about sixty five miles situated on the Delaware River. The army lay at Easton a few days & then permission was given to the company to which deponent belonged commanded by Capt. Samuel Gray to proceed to Schenectady in the State of New York as fast as they pleased. The company crossed the Delaware at Easton & proceeded through the State of New Jersey to New Windsor situated on the North River a short distance above the highlands in the State of New York. They stayed at this place a few days & then proceeded home to Stone Arabia where they arrived late in the fall.

In January following, the year 1780, deponent again enlisted to carry provisions to Fort Stanwix & other forts west of Schenectady as before stated & went to Albany in February to muster, & was then sent home to remain till the river opened in the spring, at which time deponent went to Schenectady & commenced boating, & continued in the same service most of the time till late in the fall. Samuel Gray was Captain or had command & direction of the boats, & each boat was manned by three men. During the summer the boats, three in number, as deponent believes, were on their way to Fort Stanwix & had proceeded as far as old Fort Schuyler where the City of Utica in the County of Oneida is now situated, when they were informed by a friendly Indian that Indians commanded by Brant were in ambush up the river to surprise & take the boats. The boatmen landed & picketed in a small spot of ground adjoining the bank of the river opposite their boats, to secure themselves against the attack of the Indians. They sent an express immediately to Schenectady for relief & Genl. Van Rensselaer came up the Mohawk River, collected the militia on his way & relieved them after they had been there eleven or twelve days, & guarded them safe to Fort Stanwix. In October of this year deponent was permitted to go home to Stone Arabia on furlough from Schenectady. While he was there the enemy burnt Schoharie & Caghnawaga & proceeded up the Mohawk River. Col. Brown, who commanded a small fort at Stone Arabia received orders from Genl. Van Rensselaer who was coming up the river from Schenectady, to give the enemy battle, & he would attack them in the rear. Brown marched out of the fort & attacked the enemy. Deponent & other militia of the Stone Arabia joined Brown & were in the battle. Brown fell fighting manfully & about thirty or forty of his men were also killed & the remainder retreated. Genl. Van Rensselaer did not come to the aide of Brown as he had promised. The next day deponent joined Gen, Van Rensselaer & pursued the enemy beyond Fort Herkimer & the day after returned to Stone Arabia. Within a few days deponent went to Schenectady & continued to serve as a boatman till the river closed in the fall, when deponent returned to Stone Arabia. In the winter following Col. Willett came to Fort Plain & commanded the troops & militia on the Mohawk River till the close of the war. Deponent was frequently out on scouting parties in the spring & forepart of summer.

In June Jacob Klock who resided on the Mohawk River in the (now) Town of Oppenheim in Montgomery County, & who had been a Lieutenant in the Continental Service turned Tory & went to Canada. He took with him several of his neighbors. In four weeks [from the – crossed out] said Klock & those who left with him returned with a party of Indians & Tories & Canadians. One Philip Helmer, who went to Canada with said Klock, left the enemy & informed the inhabitants of the approach of the Indians & Tories. An express [i.e. messenger] was sent to Stone Arabia on Sunday & deponent & all the militia turned out. They were joined by a company of New Levies [Willettt's State troops] under the command of Capt. Jacob Simmons & Lieutenant

Isaac Perry & went in search of the enemy. Deponent & six others sent as an advance guard & to follow the trail of the enemy. They overtook the enemy about noon, in the woods & fired upon them & killed one Indian. The enemy were resting when they were discovered & when fired upon fled & left all their packs & many left their guns & hats. One of the party scalped the Indian that was killed & Andrew Gray carried the scalp to the fort at Stone Arabia. The enemy fled immediately from the country. Deponent was frequently out on scouting parties during the summer & the first of September as he believes a party of Indians & Tories attacked a block house occupied by Jacob Timmerman in the (now) Town of Oppenheim in the said County of Montgomery. The alarm was given & the militia [& the militia – crossed out] were called out at Stone Arabia & joined Col. Willett at the block house & went in pursuit of the enemy who had fled & taken several prisoners who resided near said blockhouse & pursued them to Jerseyfield (now) the north part of the County of Herkimer & then returned home. After this & during the fall the Indians again made their appearance on the Mohawk River & killed one Foster & his family & burnt his buildings. The alarm was given & the militia turned out at Stone Arabia & pursued the enemy a day or two & then returned home. From this time till late in the fall there were alarms frequently given, parties of two and three Indians each were prowling about & whenever they were discovered or attacked the inhabitants of any part of the country the militia always turned out, & very often without finding the enemy. Several times during the following winter deponent was called out with the militia of Stone Arabia.

During the war & in the winter a settlement (now) in the Town of Fairfield in the said County of Herkimer was attacked by the Indians. Several of the inhabitants were killed & others taken prisoner & their buildings were burnt & property destroyed. Another settlement in the (now) northeast part of the County of

Herkimer was attacked by the Indians & the inhabitants were taken prisoners & their buildings & property destroyed. Deponent was out with the militia in pursuit of the enemy at both times last stated, thinks it was in the first part of the year 1782, but will not be certain. (2)

In the spring of the year 1782 deponent went with a part of his company under the command of Capt. Samuel Gray to Fort Plain, then commanded by Col. Willett. They stayed a few days at Fort Plain & then the troops under the command of Col. Willett went into the south part of the (now) County of Montgomery to a place called Bowmans Creek in pursuit of the Indians & Tories who had collected there. They fled at the approach of Willet & the troops after traversing the country for a few days they returned to Fort Plain. **From this time till the first of October deponent was [engaged – crossed out] at Fort Plain, Fort Plank about two miles west of Fort Plain, & at Fort Herkimer & with the militia traversing the country in pursuit of small parties of Indians & Tories that infested the country.** In October the British, Indians, & Tories under the Command of Major Ross & Walter Butler made their appearance on the Mohawk River in the (now) County of Montgomery. The alarm spread through the country. Deponent & two other young men started from Stone Arabia & went down the Mohawk River about twelve miles & joined Col. Willett at a place called Anthony's Nose. Willett proceeded down the south side of the river a few miles below Caghnawaga where Willett met an express who informed him the enemy was on the north side of the Mohawk River & on their way to Johnstown. Willett returned up the river & crossed over to Caghnawaga where he sent deponent & one William Wallace as a scout to ascertain the situation of the enemy. They proceeded to Johnstown & discovered the enemy a little distance west of Johnson Hall, they were building fires & encamping. Wallace returned to inform Col. Willett & deponent remained at the jail with six persons who were under the Command of one Capt. Lidle [Little], then keeper of the jail. Deponent & the company under Capt. Lidle, when they saw Col. Willett advancing, proceeded to the place where the enemy had built their fires & saw them retreating into the woods about half a mile to the north, towards Kingsborough.   Deponent & his party pursued as fast as they could run & came up close to the woods & halted.   Col. Willett sent a party of men under the command of Major Andrew Finck to join Capt. Lidles party & enter into the woods & fire upon the enemy & then retreat & bait the enemy out into the field. They entered into the woods a short distance & were fired upon by the enemy & one or two of their party [were] killed.   They returned the fire & the enemy retreated & deponent & his party pursued them about half a mile into the woods.   When they came up to the main body of the enemy deponent & Major Finck were in advance of their party & were fired upon by the enemy who stood on the top of the hill above them. The balls stuck in the tree ten or fifteen feet over deponents head. Deponent fired at an Indian not more than twenty paces distant & the Indian fell. Major Fink then called out to his men to retreat as the enemy were surrounding them & they retreated into the open field & were followed by the enemy.   Deponent & his party joined a company under the command of Capt. Moody, who had command of a cannon.   They made a stand a short time when they saw a large party of the enemy going through the woods to surround them & cut off their retreat to the town & then deponent & his party left the cannon & retreated to the town & joined Col. Willett, who had rallied his men & had received a reinforcement of militia. Willett advanced to meet the enemy & again took the cannon & the enemy were driven from the field & retreated. During the battle several of dependents friends & companions from Stone Arabia were severely wounded & deponent was requested to go to Stone Arabia to inform their friend & bring them to Johnstown to take care of the wounded.   Deponent started immediately & went [to Stone Arabia – crossed out] in the night to Stone Arabia about 12 miles & ate nothing from early in the morning till late at night when he arrived at Stone Arabia. The next morning deponent returned to

Johnstown to join Col. Willett, who deponent learned had gone in pursuit of the enemy & deponent followed Willett to Fort Herkimer & stayed at the fort one night. All the militia had gone with Willett in pursuit of the enemy & deponent returned home to Stone Arabia. This battle between the enemy & Colonel Willett at Johnstown deponent verily believes was in the fall of the year 1782 as above stated, but by many of the Revolutionary soldiers it is said this battle was fought in the fall of the year 1781 which deponent thinks is incorrect. (3)

In the winter following many of the Tories that had joined Ross & Butler at Johnstown returned home to the (now) County of Montgomery. The Whigs were so much enraged against them that they went in parties & whipped the Tories. The Tories swore the [blazes ?] of them, & the Whigs, to the number of eight or nine, went captive to jail at Johnstown. The news was brought to Stone Arabia & deponent & several others went to Johnstown, broke [into] the jail & liberated the prisoners. The same winter Jacob Klock, who had been a Lieutenant in the Continental service, & turned Tory as above mentioned, returned home about six miles from Stone Arabia. His father & Capt. Christian House sent a letter to Stone Arabia saying they would protect him to the utmost of their power. The militia of Stone Arabia were collected to go & take said Klock & they chose deponent, Samuel Gray & Isaac Paris their leaders & went to the house of said Klock's father, where he stayed & was kantoned [i.e. cantoned], but he had fled to the woods. A file of men was sent after said House & brought him to said Klock's & said House and said Klock had to beg for their lives with their hats under their armes & confess they had done wrong & promised to do better. (4)

That he is unable to obtain any witness who can testify in detail to his service and has made signed formal witness that he was born at Stone Arabia in the now County of Montgomery in the year 1756. That he has no record of his age. That when he entered the service of the United States in the Revolutionary War he resided at Amsterdam in the Palatine District in the now County of Montgomery (5) Since the Revolutionary War he resided at Stone Arabia about two years when he removed to the now Town of Little Falls in Herkimer County where he now resides.

That he rendered his first service in the militia in which he was enrolled. In 1778 he was drafted and served as in his statement related & in 1780 he volunteered to enter the service and served as a volunteer as related in his statement.

Some of the regular officers who were with the troops where he served, Colonel Willett, Colonel Gansevoort, General Clinton, Col. VanSchaick, Gen. Sullivan, Gen Poor, Gen. Hand, Gen. Maxwell, Gen. James Clinton, Surgeon Doctor Green.

That he never received a written discharge except the affidavit hereto annexed made before Peter S. Dygert a Justice of the Peace on the day of this taking and date thereof, the 14 January 1783, which affidavit is signed by Samuel Gray who was the Captain of the deponent during the war, and the others were the deponents companions in many a perilous scout upon the trail after Indians & Tories serving the term stated in said affidavit. Deponent saith that his name then & many times since has been spelled Vetter, but saith this affidavit was made for him this deponent, & has been ever since been in deponent's possession. Deponent saith that all the persons who have signed said affidavit are dead except Barent Cryser [Chrysler] who is so feeble in mind as not to remember scarcely anything.

... [Repeats information in last paragraph] ... That he is known to Peter Woolaver of the Town of Manheim & John P. Spinner minister of the gospel of the Town of Herkimer [from his neighborhood – crossed out] who can testify as to his character for veracity and their belief as to his service as a soldier of the revolution.

He hereby relinquishes every claim whatever to a pension or annuity except the present and declares that his name is not on the pension roll of the agency of any state.

Sworm to & subscribed, the day & year aforesaid in open court.

[signed] William Fater

Julius C. Nelson, Clerk

[Transcript of document submitted as evidence and mentioned above]

State of New York

That the representatives & Inhabitants of the County of Tryon testify, certify and declare upon oath that William Vetter of Palatine District and County aforesaid hath constantly and uniformly since the ninth day of July 1776 demeaned himself as a friend to freedom and indepentance of the United States and hath, as far as his circumstances would atmit taken an active and defensive part to maintain and perpetuate the same.

Sworn before me this 14 day of January 1783.

Peter S. Deygert, Justice

Samuel Gray   Martin Nesbet Conrath Kils [Kilts]
George Sprege [Spraker] Andrew Wirner [Warner]   Peter B. Young
Gerred Lesaker [Lenneker ?]   Gerele Kern   Richd. Young
Wellem Warmud [Wormuth] Barend Crysler [Chrysler] Frances Bader [Bauder]

S.13013 -- End Notes -- William Feeter
By Wayne Lenig

1. Feeter is mistaken, VanSchaick's expedition was against the *Onondaga village* not the *Oneidas*. The *Oneidas* remained allied to U.S. intrests throughout the war.

2. The two raids Feeter references in the northeastern part of what is now the Town of Manheim occurred in the late winter and early spring of 1780. The earlier raid was on March 15; the second attack came on April 3, 1780.

3. Once again the applican't's memory is faulty. The Battle of Johnstown was fought on October 25, 1781.

4. This is an interesting and rare account of enmity and coercive activities that must have occurred regulary after 1782, when loyalists attempted to return to their former

homes in the Mohawk Valley. Official documents and records rarely refer to these incidents.

5. The City of Amsterdam was actually in the Mohawk District, Tryon County, in 1776. By 1832, it was in the Town of Amsterdam, Montgomery County. Not surprisingly, 57 years later the judge who attested to this document in neighboring Herkimer County did not realize this was a mistake.

Pension Application for Francis Frederick

S.23643
State of New York
County of Otsego SS

Francis Frederick of Danube in the County of Herkimer & State aforesaid being duly sworn deposeth & Saith. That his services—in the War of the Revolution so far as he can now specify. This same were as follows. That they were under the officers set forth & described in this declaration hereunto annexed. Viz: At Sir Guy Johnsons (1) the militia being called out.	6 days
At Johnstown twenty days [sic]	20 days
With a party of Militia in pursuing from Johnstown & capturing 12 tories, out at that time	10 days
At the Fish House (Socknedaga) near Johnstown	15 days
On an alarm at Stone Arabia and going from thence to guard a lot of fat cattle from thence to Fort Stanwix	8 days
At the time the bateaux were guarded up the Mohawk River, the deponent with a	8 days

small party drove cattle on land

At Fort Plank at one time	**15 days**
At Fort Plain six times 2 days each time	**12 days**
At the Block House at Socknedaga at one time	15 days
At the same place at another time	10 days
At Van Alstine's on the Mohawk	5 days
At the time of the Oriskany Battle near Fort Stanwix (2)	16 days
At Caughnawaga at the time of the wounding of Col. Fisher six days (3)	6 days
At the time of the burning of Schoharie Settlement	12 days
Keeping garrison at Stone Arabia (4)	19 days
At Johnstown when the troops were esconded from that place	15 days
At Tripes Hill at one time	15 days
At Johnstown in the year in which independence was declared, previous to that above mentioned	15 days
At Fort Herkimer on an alarm Major Fonda being there	8 days

End Notes -- S.23643—Francis Frederick

1. Guy Johnson's home still stands in Amsterdam, N.Y. It is a New York State Historical Site. Guy Johnson was a nephew and son-in-law to Sir William Johnson. Guy was also a colonel in the British Indian Department.
2. The Battle of Oriskany was fought on the 6th of August 1777.
3. Caughnawaga and Tribes Hill were destroyed on the 22nd of May 1780 by Sir John Johnson, son of Sir William Johnson. John's Town was named by Sir William for his son John. It originally was two words.
4. Fort Paris is the fort where he would have been stationed.

5. Captain Samuel Pettingill of the Fifth Company. Thomas Caine was first lieutenant and Samuel Barnhardt, Jr. was the ensign. The second lieutenant was blank or vacant in August of 1775. Sometime in 1776 William Snook was appointed the second lieutenant and received his commission dated 25 June 1778. Thomas Van Horne was the Ensign with the same timeline as Snook. After the Battle of Oriskany, William Snook was appointed Captain, Thomas Van Horne First Lieutenant, Peter Young was Second Lieutenant and Conradt Stine was Ensign. All were commissioned on the 8th of March 1781.

6. Francis's name appears also in Captain Robert A. Yates' Company (Third Company) in Colonel Visscher's Regiment. As Francis did not move and each company had a particular area of enrollment this is probably for a draft of men fromvarious companies to form a detachment to perform a particular duty. The date is unknown.

Pension Application for Ebenezer French

S.13090

State of New York

Ontario Countty SS

On this twenty-seventh day of August 1832, personally appeared in open court before the Judges of the County Court now sitting Ebenezer French a resident of the Town of Bloomfield County and State aforesaid aged seventy two years who being duly sworn according to law doth on his oath make the following declaration in order to obtain the benefit of the Act of Congress passed June 7, 1832.

That he entered the service of the United States under the following named officers and served as herein stated.

1st At the Town of Killingworth State of Connecticut was drafted for one month in Captain Samuel Gales Company in Colonel Worthington's Regiment in October 1777 was marched to Fish Kill and then to Red Hook under General Putnam and was a guard near him and knew him well, went back to Fish Kill and when his time expired he was discharged at Fishkill and went home.

2nd   At the same place in the month of October 1778 was drafted in Captain Gilbert Dudley's Company for one month and was marched to Roger's Neck near New London and served at the time at that place keeping guard, there was no other company there and we were doing duty at this place.

3rd   About the 1st November 1779 at the same place was drafted for two months in Captain Kelsey's Company Major Commandant Smith and marched to New Haven and then to Stratford and after a short time was ordered back to New Haven and there done duty until he time expired and then went home to Killingsworth.

4th   In June 1780 his father moved to Alford in Massachusetts and he this declarant enlisted in July 1780 at Alford in Captain Warner's (1) Company in Colonel Brown's (2) Regiment and was marched to Claverack and thence to Albany then to Fort Plain on the Mohawk then to Herkimer then to Fort Stanwix and served in this campaign three months and was discharged at Fort Plank near Fort Plain and went home having served three months Colonel Dubois was there.

5th   At Alford as aforesaid in July 1781 he enlisted again in Captain Jeremiah (3) Heacoxe? Company and was ordered to Fort Plain and was under the Command of Colonel Willett (4) and served at Fort Plain and Herkimer and other places on this station but most part of the time at Fort Plain and served three months, and after my time was out he joined Captain Skinner's (5) Company at the same place and served one month and after this was discharged and went home to Alford.

6th   Besides the foregoing he was called out on short tours of duty and was out at Derby in April 1777, then to New Haven, and when the British landed at New Haven was called out and when he got to East Haven the British returned to their ships. The British cut down the Beacon at East Haven at this time. He believes he served in three short tours in all half a month and he served his country in all during the War of the Revolution thirteen months and a half. Has no documentary evidence. Christopher Parks, Marvin Gates, knows of his service. Was born in Guilford Connecticut 11th October 1760 at the age of 9 years moved to Killingsworth then to Alford and from Alford to Bloomfield in the year 1798 and has lived there until now.

He hereby relinquishes every claim whatever to a pension or annuity except the present and declared his name is not on the pension roll of the agency of any other state. (Signed) Ebenezer French

End Notes -- S.13090 -- Ebenezer French

1. Captain Samuel Warner
2. Colonel John Brown's Regiment of Massachusetts State Levies
3. Captain Jeremiah Hickock's Company in Colonel Elisha Porter's Regiment of Massachusetts State Levies.
4. The Massachusetts Levies marched to the Mohawk River under Major Aaron Rowley from Porter's Regiment. Colonel Marinus Willet was the overall commander of the troops in the Mohawk Valley at this time.
5. French's name does not appear on the payroll for Captain Thomas Skinner's Company in Colonel Willett's Regiment.

Pension Application for Peter Marsh

W.19856 (Dorothy Maybee/Mabee, Widow)
State of New York
Peter Marsh, (aka) John Thomas Trantum, was born in London England
County of Onondaga SS.

On this 4th day of December in the year of our Lord one thousand eight hundred and thirty eight personally appeared before the Judges of the Court of Common Pleas in and for the

County of Onondaga in open court, Dorothy Marsh a resident of the Town of Manlius in said County of Onondaga and State of New York aged seventy six years, who being first duly sworn according to law doth on her oath make the following declaration in order to obtain the benefit of the provision made by the Act of congress passed July 7th 183[?].

That she was married to Peter Marsh who was in the Revolutionary Army under different officers and at different places about seven years and was two years a sergeant under Colonel Willet (1) and while in such service marched to Fort Stony and to Oswego and to other places the names of which deponent cannot now remember. That while in such service he was shot through the thigh and wounded in the leg. That he was in the service about two months after his marriage to deponent, and in his life time frequently told deponent that he was in a battle but deponent is unable to state what battle deponent is also unable to state whether there is any documentary evidence of such service at the department or not and that she has no such evidence in her possession. She further declares that she was married to the said Peter Marsh in the month of October in the year of our Lord one thousand seven hundred and eighty three. That her husband the aforesaid Peter Marsh died on the eleventh day of March in the year of our Lord one thousand eight hundred and twenty one. And that she has remained a widow ever since that period as will more fully appear by reference to the proof hereunto annexed. (Signed with her mark) Dorothy Marsh.

Subscribed and sworn to before Gron Lawrence, First Judge of Onondaga County.

State of New York
Onondaga County SS.

John Thomas Trantum of the Town of Columbus, County of Warren & State of Pennsylvania being duly sworn deposeth & saith that he will be sixty six years of age on the first day of

November next having been born on the first day of November 1781 as appears from his family record made by himself more than forty years ago, and as has always been represented to him by his father. That he is a son of Peter Marsh who died upwards of twenty six years ago in the Town of Manlius in said county of Onondaga. Deponent is now upon a visit to his brother Nicholas Marsh who still lives in said Town of Manlius. And deponent further saith that is father's true name was also John Thomas Trantum. Deponent has often been informed by his said father and by many others who were conversant with the fact, that his said father was a British soldier, and came to this country with the British troops at or near the commencement of the war of the revolution. That he deserted from the British when the army was quartered upon Rhode Island, a short time previous to the capture of Major Prescott by Colonel Barton. That after desertion he proceeded to the American camp and was hailed by a sentry there on guard, and taken into custody by him. That this sentry, whose name was Joseph Wilbur, afterwards conducted him to his father's house in Plainfield, Connecticut, where he afterwards made it his home. Said Joseph Wilbur was deponent's uncle from whom deponent has often received these facts. That afterwards said John Thomas Trantum, deponent's father as aforesaid, enlisted into the American Army from Plainfield aforesaid, for during the war. Deponent remembers the name of Capt. Durkee among the officers under whom his said father served. He then, to avoid detection, changed his name from Trantum to that of Peter Marsh by which he was ever afterwards known. That while in said service his said father married Happy Wilbur, a sister of said Joseph Wilbur in whose father's family he had been adopted. That this deponent was his first and only son by said Happy Wilbur who continued to live in her father's family & in Plainfield aforesaid until her death. That deponent's father was in the service aforesaid when deponent was born. Shortly afterwards visiting home to see his family he desired that deponent's name should be called after his own, to wit, John Thomas Trantum. He has since often requested deponent to continue the name in the family, and in accordance with his wishes deponent's oldest son and grandson both bear the name of John Thomas Trantum.

That before the close of the war of the revolution & while he was still in service as aforesaid deponent's father the said John Thomas Trantum alias Peter Marsh was again married to Dorothy Maybee of the Town of Fort Plain & state of New York— **That he was thus married while on duty upon the Mohawk River where he often stated that he served about six months near the close of said war & that during this service Colonel Willett of New York State was chief in command at the various frontier forts on said river to wit, Fort Plain, Fort Plank, fort Stanwix, Stone Arabia &c.** He did not, to Deponent's knowledge ever enlist under Colonel Willett as has been supposed. He belonged to the Connecticut Line into which he had enlisted as aforesaid from Plainfield, Connecticut & in which he was promoted to the rank of sergeant, as he and others have often stated. He was under Colonel Willett's command as the general officer of all the forts along the Mohawk during the year he served there. Deponent continued to live in Plainfield, Connecticut & most of the time with his grandfather Wilbur until he was thirty years of age. His father the said Peter Marsh lived in Fort Plain & afterwards in Manlius, New York where he raised a family of children by his second wife the said Dorothy Maybee. All the above facts which occurred before deponent's recollection deponent has often heard related by his said father, by his said uncle Joseph Wilbur who died before the pension laws were passed & by another uncle whose name was Oliver Wilbur who died in the receipt of a pension at Delhi, New York, said Oliver served with deponent's father & as deponent believes in the same company & regiment. (Signed) John T. Trantum

Subscribed & sworn this 17th day of September 1847--& I certify that said John Thomas Trantum is a credible witness. R. Gilmor, J. Peace

End Notes for Peter Marsh W19856

1. According to The Regimental Descriptive Book No 4, for Colonel Marinus Willett's Regiment, Document No. 11105, Special Collections and Manuscripts, New York State Library, Albany NY, Peter entered the service as a substitute for Thomas Watts on January 18, 1783. His residence was in Plainfield, Windham County, Connecticut. He stated he was born at Campo, Fairfield County, Connecticut. His age was 22, size 5 ft 5 in, complexion-light, hair-black, eyes-gray, and occupation was smith. His term of service was for 1 year 4 months and 14 days. Marsh had served as a private in Captain Job Wright's Company in Colonel Willett's Regiment. A Peter Marsh was a sergeant in Captain Jonathan Pearce's Company in Colonel Willett's Regiment in 1783. He served 12 months, was paid £40..0..0 and owed £80..0..0 FROM: Series M-246, Roll 78, Folder 173, National Archives, Washington DC.

Pension Application for John McGraw

S11051

State of New York

Montgomery County

On the nineteenth day of September in the year of our Lord one thousand eight hundred and thirty two personally appeared in open court before the judges of the Court of Common Pleas of the County & State aforesaid now sitting at Johnstown, John McGraw, aged eighty years. Who being first duly sworn according to law doth on his oath make the following declaration in order to obtain the benefit of the act of Congress passed June 7, 1832. That he entered the service of the United States under the following named officers and served as herein stated.

That in the latter part of the year 1775, this deponent belonged to a company of Militia in the Town of Florida in the County and State aforesaid whereof Samuel Pettingell (1) was Captain in a Regiment commanded by Col. Frederick Fisher (Visscher) of the New York State Militia. That this deponent received orders from his captain to prepare himself with a gun, bayonet and cartridge box to fight for liberty and freedom.

That this deponent prepared himself accordingly and sometime in the forepart of the year 1776 as near as he can recollect, he was drafted from Captain Pettingell's company to go to Sacandaga at a Block House (3) built by the Americans at this place for the purpose of preventing the Tories, British &hostile Indians from passing to and from this part of the country to Canada.

That this deponent with William Snook the Lieutenant of the Company and Henry Snook, William Pettingell, Joseph Pettingell, Daniel MdGraw & Hugh Connolly privates in said company and probably others which he does not now remember, marched from the Town of Florida to Sacandaga and lay in the fort as a guard at that place until relieved by another draft from the same company.

That he had been drafted and went to Sacandaga four or five times in like manner and served his several tours at that place, sometimes would be stationed there a week, at others a fortnight, three weeks and a month, as occasions in the service required, but he cannot be particular as to the precise time he did serve there, he judges however, that he served in all the Sacandaga Block House as much as two months at least.

That in going from Florida to Sacandaga they usually crossed the Mohawk River at Tripes Hill, and some times at Amsterdam, and marched to the Block House at Sacandaga principally through the woods and that place as but little improvement in roads had been made, to that section of country as well as to avoid any surprises by the enemy.

And this deponent further says, that in the year 1777 he was drafted in like manner from Captain Pettengill's Company as many as five times and served regular tours at Johnstown in a picket fort around the Johnstown Jail.

That the several times of service at that place would vary from one to four and five weeks before he got relieved.

That Captain Walter Vrooman (3) commanded at the fort a principle part of the time.

That one Beekman (4) was Lieutenant and one Hatch a Sergeant.

That the object in keeping a force at that place was that the Americans apprehended an attack from the enemy coming through from Canada by the way of Sacandaga, Johnstown being the residence of Sir John Johnson, a Tory who had done much injury during the war.

That in the month of August 1777 Captain Pettingell's company was ordered out and the whole of Col. Fisher's Regiment to March for Oriskany in the County of Oneida at the time the battle was fought between the Americans and the British at that place and that this deponent was excused from serving at that place in consequence of a lame knee.

That in the Oriskany Battle Captain Pettingill was mortally wounded as this deponent was informed and believes, and Lieutenant Snook (5) afterwards took command of the company and was appointed captain.

That after the Oriskany Battle a certain number was drafted from Captain Snook's Company to join General Gates (6) forces at Saratoga, among which was this deponent, that one Thomas Van Horne (7) commanded the draft from same company, he the being Lieutenant of said company.

That they marched from Florida to the City of Schenectady and from thence down the Mohawk River and crossed over into Saratoga near Stillwater and there found General Gates Army.

And a few days before the battle between the forces commanded by General Gates, and those of the British commanded by General Burgoyne, this deponent was ordered to the town of Florida on business by Major David McMaster (8) who commanded the forces at Stillwater to which this deponent was attached in the Militia. And this deponent did not return as this news arrived, that the battle had been fought and that Burgoyne and his army had been taken.

And this deponent further says that sometime in the year 1778 as near as he can recollect, Col. Fisher's Regiment was ordered out including Captain Snook's Company & marched to Stone Arabia in the Town of Palatine upon an alarm of hostilities in that quarter, and were there about ten days as near as he could judge and was then relieved by another company of militia.

That in the year 1779 this deponent was drafted from Captain Snook's Company to march to the German Flats. He recollects that Captain Snook was among the number and that Robert McCrady, Cornelius Van Horne, William Phillips, Daniel McGraw, Conradt Steen, Justin Rorey and Henry Snook, privates in said company were also among the number drafted.

That they marched up the Mohawk River on the south side to the German Flats and joined some Militia at that place, who had been called out in consequence of the Indians having scalped some of the Americans at that place. That this deponent was then absent about three weeks.

That this deponent had been ordered out in the years 1778, 1779, and 1780 on various occasions and stationed at Fort Plain, Fort Plank, Fort Windecker, Fort Dayton and the German Flats to protect the Americans from the incursions of the British and Indians. That from the repeated and number of occasions this deponent had been called and stationed at the before mentioned places in the American service, and from the great length of time, he is unable to state particularly how long he served in each of those places in particular. He recollects that he has been at Bowman's Creek in the Town of Canajoharie and served on regular tour on guard at that place.

That at the time the battle was fought at Johnstown between the American forces commanded by Col. Willett and the British troops then commanded by Major Ross (9), Captain Snook's company was ordered out and went to their relief and arrived the next morning after the battle was over and thinks that the Americans followed Major Ross about two days journey, Major Ross marched westward towards The Canada Creek but that Capt Snooks Company joined the Americans and pursued Ross as before mentioned and then returned.

This deponent further says that he has been stationed at Tripes Hill to stand guard at that place, an attack was expected from the Tories, he cannot remember the year but thinks it was the latter part of the war, nor the length of time, but he remembers that Captain Snook Commanded at the time.

Captain Snook's (10) Company was also called out sometime the latter part of the war, and was stationed opposite Fort Plain in the now Town of Oppenheim (now St. Johnsville) as he believes on the north side of the Mohawk River and helped guard at that place.

They crossed the Mohawk River a little above Caughnawaga & marched up the river on the north side and found some of the American commanded by one McMasters, he cannot recollect how long they were stationed there.

He has also been placed on guard at a stone house a little below Fort Hunter to watch the movements of the Tories & Indians but how long, cannot recollect.

And this deponent further says that during the whole war he held himself in readiness to march any moment he was called upon to serve his country, and from the various services which rendered he thinks he can safely state that he served the country as much as two years and probably much longer, but his memory fails him and he cannot detail the events of the war with much minuteness or exactness.

And this deponent further says that he was born in the town of Florida in the County and state aforesaid in the year 1752 and resided in the same place when he entered the service and has so resided ever since. That he has a record of his age in his family Bible written in German in his possession, that when called into service he had been principally drafted or called upon by his superior officers and always held himself in readiness to obey the call and served the country on his own account that he has stated the names of the principle officers engaged in the services as near as he can recollect and the circumstances of his services. He has no documentary evidence in his possession nor any written discharge and hereby relinquishes every claim whatever to a pension or annuity except the present, and declare that his name is not on the pension roll of the agency of any state or of the United States and this deponent expects to prove by Henry Snevt, Garret Newkirk, Daniel McGraw & George Stine some of his services He also expects to prove by Nicholas Hill & Henry Snook who can testify as to the veracity of this deponent and of their belief as to this deponent's services as soldier of the Revolution. (Signed with his mark) John McGraw

Sworn to and subscribed this day and year aforesaid, Geo D. Ferguson, Clerk.

End Notes-- S11051--John McGraw

1. Pettingill was Captain of the Fifth Company in Col. Frederick Visscher's Regiment of Tryon County Militia [Third Regiment].
2. The service at the Sacandaga Blockhouse was in 1779 or later. However there were earthen redoubts in or near the same area as early as 1776.
3. In 1780, Walter Vrooman was a Captain in Colonel John Harper's Regiment of New York State Levies.

4. The lieutenant was John Bateman and the sergeant was William Hatch.

5. William Snook became Captain but was not commissioned until the 8th of March 1781. John mentions Henry Snook who is the son of William Snook and Daniel McGraw is John's brother.

6. Major General Horatio Gates.

7. Thomas Van Horne was the Ensign and received his Commission dated 25 June 1778. He was promoted to First Lieutenant and received his commission on 8 March 1781.

8. David McMaster was the captain of the Sixth Company in Colonel Visscher's Regiment.

9. The Battle of Johnstown was fought on the 25 of October 1781. The British were led by Major John Ross and Captain Walter Butler.

10. John also is listed as serving as a private in Captain Hermanus Mabee's Company in Colonel Visscher's Regiment.

Pension Application for Lodowick Moyer, also known as Lewis Mayer, Myer, Meyer, etc.

S.11115

State of New York

County of Herkimer SS.

On this eleventh day of February in the year 1833 personally appeared in Open Court before the Judges of the Court of Common Pleas of the said County of Herkimer the same being a Court of Record having by Law a clerk & seal now setting Lodowick Moyer a resident of the Town of Fairfield in the said County of Herkimer & State of New York aged Seventy years and upwards who being first duly sworn according to Law doth on his oath make the following declaration in order to obtain the benefit of the Act of Congress passed June 7, 1832, That he entered the service of the United States under the following named officers and served as herein stated--:

In the Year 1778 said Lodowick Moyer resided on the Royal Grant or Kingsland now in the Town of Little Falls in the County of Herkimer then in the County of Tryon in the State of New York and Early in the Spring as he believes about the first of April 1778 he this deponent enlisted as a substitute for Henry Shaffer his stepfather at Kingsland aforesaid into Capt. McKeans (1) Company for Nine months & was marched to Fort Drayton[Dayton] in Germanflatts on the north side of the Mohawk river & was stationed at said Fort a short time and from thence he was sent with a small party of men to Fort Mike (2) in Germanflatts now the Town of Schuyler in said County on the North side of the Mohawk river & he this deponent was stationed with said party of men under the immediate command of Sergeant John Siver who was the Sergeant in Capt. McKeans Company to guard the inhabitants & their property against the enemy and he this deponent was employed at said Fort Mike in scouting, driving fat cattle to Fort Stanwix; standing on sentry and scouring the country around about in search of Indians and Tories and the continued to serve at said station as above stated until his time expired and he this deponent served in Captain McKeans Company as aforesaid nine months—And this deponent further saith that he does not remember the name of the Col of the Regiment to which Capt. McKeans Company was attached unless it was Col. Van Rensselaer and he cannot say certainly as he was Colonel as he this deponent did not serve the above time in any Regiment under the immediate command of a Colonel—

And this deponent further saith that after serving nine months as aforesaid he was discharged sometime in the winter and as he thinks in the last of December 1778 or the forepart of January following but he received no discharge in writing—The officers under whom he served were Capt. McKean Lieut. Smith

(3) who had the active command of the company—Sergeant Sivers.

And this deponent further saith that in the Spring & he believes about the first of April 1779 he this deponent enlisted as a volunteer at Fort Plank now in the Town of Minden in Montgomery County into Capt. Bradpick's (4) Company in the State service for nine months and he was marched to Fort Plain and after remaining at said Fort a short time he was sent on command with a small party to Col. Veeder's Block Mills in Cathnewaga [Caughnawaga] & was stationed at the said Block Mills in the state guards and he served in said guards and on Sentry; in scouting and defending the inhabitants & their property against the Indians & Tories, who made frequent inroads upon the settlements at that time in that section of the Country— And this deponent further saith that he served as above stated nine months and he was discharged from the service in the latter part of December 1779 or the forepart of January following but he took no discharge in writing. The officers under whom he served were Capt. Bradpick, Lieut. Helmer; Sergeant Ohrendorff (5) frequently took command of small parties who were sent out to scour the Country—And this deponent saith that he cannot say who was the Colonel of the Regiment to which Capt. Bradpick's Company belonged as he their deponent did not serve in any Regiment under the immediate Command of a Colonel.

And this deponent further saith that Early in the Spring and he believes about the first of April 1780 he this deponent enlisted as a volunteer at Fort Plank aforesaid into Capt. Bradpick's (6) Company in Col. Van Rensselaer's (7) Regiment in the State service for nine months and he was stationed for some time at Fort Herkimer & from thence he was marched with the company under the Command of Capt. Bradpick to Stone Arabia and stationed at Keyser's Block House and he was employed at said station in scouting & standing sentry & this deponent further saith that he was marched with the company under Capt.

Bradpick to Palatine to meet the enemy and that a battle ensued between The American forces under the Command of Col. Van Rensselaer (8) and the Indians and Tories commanded as was said by Col. Butler & Sir John Johnson –This battle was fought in a field called Failing's Orchard on the north side of the Mohawk river and he this deponent was engaged in the battle under the Command of Capt. Bradpick and was stationed with one division of the American Troops on a hill where they fought—The enemy gave way and fled across the river and retreated to the west as was said but this deponent did not follow in pursuit—And this deponent further saith that he served nine months and was discharged in the latter part of December 1780 or the forepart of January following but he received no discharge in writing—the officers under whom he served were Capt. Bradpick Lieut Coppernoll (9) Col. Willett. (10)

And this deponent further saith that early in the Spring and he believes the first of April 1781 he this deponent enlisted as a volunteer at Fort Plank aforesaid into Capt. Putman's (11) company in Col. Willett's Regiment in the State service for nine months and he was stationed at Fort Plank and then at Fort Plain and stood Sentry and was sent out in scouting and afterwards he was marched with the company under the Command of Capt. Putman to Johnstown along with Col. Willetts Regiment and the British Indians & Tories had appeared there in a considerable force and a battle followed which was fought near Johnstown between the forces under the Command of Col. Willett and the Enemy commanded as was said by Col. Walter Butler & Maj. Ross (12) –And this deponent saith that he was engaged in this battle with the Company under the Command of Capt. Putman and the Enemy were routed and made them retreat up the north side of the Mohawk river—Col. Willetts Regiment pursued the Enemy in their flight and this deponent was placed in charge of some prisoners, who were taken on their retreat—This deponent pursued the enemy with Col. Willett's Regiment & arrived at West Canada Creek (13) where the Enemy had crossed, shortly after Col. Butler was shot on the opposite bank by an Oneida Indian— The Indian immediately forded the creek & came up to Butler and in spite of his entreaties dispatched him as the story was told with his Tomahawk on the spot—This deponent felt no pity for Butler who it was said was one who led on the massacre of the inhabitants of Cherry Valley—And this deponent further saith that Col. Willetts Regiment followed the Enemy about a day after crossing West Creek in hopes to take them but the weather was bad & stormy and being short of provisions they were unable to go farther in the pursuit and Col. Willett ordered his Regiment to return and after undergoing much fatigue & suffering by cold & hunger they arrived back upon the Mohawk river (14) & this deponent was stationed with Capt. Putman's Company at Fort Plain & employed in scouting and standing Sentry until he was discharged—And he this deponent served as above stated nine months in the Year 1781 and was discharged in the last of December 1781 or the forepart of January following but he received no discharge in writing except that Col. Willett gave him as he thinks a written discharge of which he is not certain but if he did the said discharge has been lost or destroyed—The officers under whom this deponent served were Capt. Putman, Lieut. Putman (15) who was a brother of Capt. Putman; Col. Willett.

And this deponent further saith that early in the spring & he believes the first of April 1782 he this deponent enlisted as a volunteer at Fort Plank aforesaid into Capt. Putman's (16) Company on Col. Willett's Regiment in the state service for nine months and he was stationed at Fort Plain in Capt. Putman's Company and served on Sentry and was frequently sent out with small parties to scour the country in search of the Indians & Tories and that he this deponent served nine months under the command of Capt. Putman & was discharge in the latter part of December 1782 as he believes but received no discharge in writing. The officers under whom he served were Capt. Putman Lieut. Putman Col. Willett.

And this deponent further saith that he was born at Freshwiller in Germany on the sixth day of July in the Year 1762.—

He had a record of his age in his Bible at his home in Fairfield aforesaid.—

He was living at Kingsland now Town of Little Falls in the said County of Herkimer when he was first called into the service in 1778 & when he was called into the service in the years 1779, 1780, 1781, & 1782 he was living near Fort Plank now in the Town of Minden Montgomery County & State of New York and since the Revolutionary War he resided in Fairfield in Herkimer County aforesaid eight or nine years & next in Manheim in said County of Herkimer a number of years & then he returned back to Fairfield aforesaid and has resided where he now resides in said Town about fifteen years now last past. And this deponent further saith that Peter Mower, Jacob Widrig, William Kisner served with this deponent in the war of the Revolution & knows that this deponent served in said war as they have stated in their respective affidavits.

And this deponent further saith that there were no regular officers who were with the troops where he served that the recollects except Col. Willett and except in the battle at Johnstown in 1781 he saw regular officers but he was not acquainted with them & he does now [not] recollect their names— And this deponent further saith that the following are the names of persons to whom he is known in this present neighborhood viz. William Feeter & Hiram Nolton who can testify as to his character for truth & veracity & their belief of his services as a Revolutionary Soldier—And this deponent saith that there is no clergyman living in his neighborhood—

He hereby relinquishes every claim whatever to a pension or an annuity except the present and he declares that his name is not on the pension roll of the agency of any State. (Signed with his mark) Lodowick Moyer

Sworn in open court Feby 11th 1833 Julius T. Wilson Clerk

End Notes—S.11115—Lodowick Moyer

1. This was actually in the year of 1779. Captain Robert McKean was appointed captain in April of 1779 in Lieutenant Colonel Commandant Henry K. VanRensselaer's Regiment of New York State Levies. A muster or payroll for this company has not been located.

2. Fort Mike was the blockhouse at or near New Germantown, now Town of Schuyler, Herkimer County.

3. Lieutenant John Smith was appointed in April of 1779. Sergeant John Sever could be John Seeber.

4. John Breadbake was appointed Captain in 1778 of a company of Rangers. Lieutenant John Adam Frederick Helmer was appointed to serve in this company.

5. Lodowick's name nor a Sergeant Ohrendorf or Ahrendorf, Olendorf, etc., are not found on Captain Breadbake's Company pay rolls from July to October 1778. This company was attached to Colonel Morris Graham's Regiment. FROM: Revolutionary War Rolls 1775-1783, Series, M-246, Roll 74, folder 106, National Archives, Washington, D.C.

6. Captain Breadbake in April of 1780 was still in Colonel Klock's Regiment. On July 1, 1780, Captain Breadbake was appointed to command a company in Colonel Lewis DuBois Regiment of New York State Levies. Lodowick is shown as Lewis Myer as enlisting on July 25 and discharged on October 24, 1780. FROM: Revolutionary War Rolls 1775-1783, Series M-246, Roll 72, folder 96.

7. Henry K. VanRensselaer did not command a regiment of levies after 1779. He actually was the lieutenant colonel of Colonel Stephen J. Schuyler's Sixth Regiment of Albany

County Militia. On March 26, 1781, Colonel Schuyler resigned and VanRensselaer commanded the regiment.

8. Lodowick at this time is referring to Brigadier General Robert VanRensselaer who commanded the American troops at the Battle of Klocksfield which was fought on October 19, 1780.

9. John Coppernoll served as a lieutenant in Captain Breadbake's Company in Colonel DuBois' Regiment in 1780.

10. Marinus Willett in 1780 was the lieutenant colonel commandant of the Fifth New York Continental Regiment. Willett nor the regiment were in the Mohawk Valley in 1780. They were at or near West Point, N.Y.

11. Captain Garret Putman's Company in Lieutenant Colonel Commandant Marinus Willett's Regiment of New York State Levies in 1781.

12. Major John Ross and Captain Walter Butler commanded the British forces at the Battle of Johnstown. This battle was fought on October 25, 1781.

13. The Skirmish at West Canada Creek on October 30, 1781. Walter Butler's father John Butler was the lieutenant colonel of Butler's Rangers. Willett mentions in his official report of Butler's death that his commission that was found in his pocket was that of a Captain. Willett also states that Butler was still alive when found.

14. Jeptha R. Simms interviewed Lodowick and used his information in Volume 2 of The Frontiersmen of New York including the West Canada Creek skirmish.

15. Lieutenant Victor Putman. Putman's Company was discharged on December 31, 1781. On Captain Putman's Receipt Roll, Lodowick had £10. . 0. . 10 owed to him and was delivered to Jellis Fonda. FROM: Revolutionary War Rolls 1775-1783, Series M-246, Roll 78, folder 173, National Archives, Washington, D.C.

16. Garret Putman was not appointed a captain in Willett's Regiment in 1782 or 1783. Victor Putman was appointed lieutenant and commissioned as such on July 24, 1782. He served in Captain Abner French's Company in 1782. Lodowick may have served in this company but so far a muster or pay roll has not been located for this company.

Pension Application for Richard Putman

W.16686

Declaration

In order to obtain the benefit of the Section of the act of Congress of the 4th July 1836

State of New York

Montgomery County SS.

On this second day of June 1837, personally appeared before the under named a Judge of the County Courts in and for the county of Montgomery aforesaid Nelly Putman a resident of the town of Johnstown—County & State aforesaid aged Eighty Seven years past, who being first duly sworn according to law, doth on her oath make the following declaration in order to obtain the benefit of the provision made by the act of Congress passed July 4, 1836. That she is the widow of Richard Putman who was a private in the war of the Revolution—in Col. Frederick Fisher's Regiment and Captain John Davis' (1) Company from the year 1775 until in August 1777—and did duty in said war at various times and places in said State—and at the Oriscany [Oriskany] battle in said state. The said Captain John Davis was killed and her husband the said Richard Putman was appointed Ensign under the command of Captain Abraham Veeder (2) in said regiment until the close of said War—but that she this applicant has no great personal knowledge of the service of her said husband but from traditionary evidence or such as was related to her at different times during said war—and since by her said husband and others, and which she believes to be true—That (the said) the said Richard Putman served as a private in said war in the militia under said Capt. Davis at Caughnawaga in the year 1775 upwards of one week—the same year under said Capt. at different other places in said County, at least about one month in the year 1776 he was with the militia on duty under said Capt. when Sir John Johnson was disarmed & that one week in then said last mentioned year under said Capt he was at Sockendaga [Sacondaga] and in the tory settlement in service and on duty at least one month. **Same year under same Capt at Stonearabia Bowmans Creek or Kill—Fort Plain and Fort Plank in service and on duty not less than one month—in the year 1777 he was out on duty in said war under said Capt. at Balstown said state at least 10 days**—same year under General Herkimer on a conference with Capt. Brant to the Unadilla (3) said state, on service at least fourteen days—the same year at the Oriscany Battle under said Capt & said Genl Herkimer on duty at least one month in the fall off same year he served and done duty in said war as Ensign in the militia against General Burgoyne (4) and before the surrender of said General Burgoyne at least six weeks in the year 1778 he did duty as Ensign in said Company at Stonearabia at least ten days—Same year as Ensign (5) **duty & was in service at the Sackendaga Block house at least one month in the fall of same year he did duty & service as Ensign at Fort Plain & Fort Plank at least three weeks,** and she further states on her oath aforesaid that she never knew or heard of her said husband staying at home or refusing or neglecting to go on duty or service at any time when the militia of said Country was ordered out on any occasion in said war but (that) that she cannot now recollect the various times when he was called out or the various places where he went on duty & service in said war—but believes that the whole amount of time he lost in during duty tour services in said war would exceed two years—She further declares that she was married to the said Richard Putman on or about the 17th day of October 1767 (6)—that her husband the aforesaid Richard Putman died on the 14th day of April 1833 (7)—and that she has remained a widow ever since that period as will more fully appear by reference to the proof hereto annexed. (Signed with her mark) Nelly Putman

Sworn to and Subscribed on the day & year aforesaid written before me John Hand a Judge of the Montgomery County Courts.

[She was granted pension of $63.11 per annum.]

I Jacob G. Snell Town Clerk of the Town of Palatine County of Montgomery and State of New York. Do certify that upon examination of the Church Records, I find recorded the marriage of Richard Putman to Nelly VanBracklen. They were married on the 17th day of October A.D. 1767 By the Rev'd Abraham Rosencrantz. Dated April 29th 1837. Jacob P. Snell J. Clerk.

Sworn and Subscribed this 29th day of April 1837. John T. Getman Justice.

End Notes—W.16686—Richard (Derick) Putman

1. John Davis was appointed Captain of the Second company on August 26, 1775 in Colonel Frederick Visscher's Third Regiment of Tryon County Militia.

2. Upon Captain Davis being killed at the Battle of Oriskany on August 6, 1777, First Lieutenant Abraham Veeder was appointed Captain of the company. Richard was actually appointed sergeant. Richard was appointed ensign in 1778 or 1779. Captain Veeder, First Lieutenant Nicholas Dockstader; Second Lieutenant, Garret S. VanBracklen or VanBrocklin; and Ensign Putman were all commissioned on March 8, 1781.

3. The conference between Captain Joseph Brant and Brigadier General Nicholas Herkimer was held June 27, 1777 at Unadilla.

4. Lieutenant General John Burgoyne surrendered his army of British troops and allies on October 17, 1777.

5. Richard continued to serve in the militia after the War of Independence. In 1784 Tryon County's name was changed to Montgomery Count. On October 2, 1786, Derick Putman was appointed Lieutenant in Captain Jacob Sammons Company (Fourth Company) in Lieutenant Colonel Commandant Volkert Veeder's Regiment of Montgomery County Militia in Brigadier General Frederick Visscher's (or Fisher) Brigade. FROM: Military Minutes of the Council of Appointments of the State of New York, ed. Hugh Hastings, Albany NY 1901, Vol. I, P 101.

6. Richard and Nelly had the following children: Cornelia born December 8, 1773, bapt on January 1, 1774. Caughnawaga Dutch Reformed Church Book of Baptisms page 27. Gerrit born on December 6, 1776 bapt on January 5, 1777, Caughnawaga Dutch Reformed Church Book of Baptisms page 40. Maria born September 12, 1779 bapt October 12, 1779 Caughnawaga Dutch Reformed Church Book of Baptisms book page 53. Lewis born April 27, 1783 bapt May 24, 1783 Caughnawaga Dutch Reformed Church Book of Baptisms page 66. Johannis born January 19, 1786 bapt March 6, 1786 Caughnawaga Dutch Reformed Church Book of Baptisms page 77. There may have been more children but these are the ones that were baptized by Reverend Thomas Romeyn.

7. Richard and Nelly are buried in the Keck Center Cemetery, Town of Johnstown, Fulton County. The cemetery is on the New Turnpike Road. Nelly died on February 20, 1842 at the age of 100 years and 7 months. Richard is the son of Lodowick and Elizabeth Soets Putman. Lodowick and his son Aaron were killed on May 22, 1780. There is an historic marker on the corner of Route 29 and the Hales

Mills Road to mark the site of the Putman Home and burial of Lodowick and Aaron.

Pension Application for John VanAntwerp

W.19897 (Widow: Rachel)
State of New York
Montgomery County SS.

On this 25th day of September 1837 personally appeared before me Myndert Starin a Commissioner of Deeds in and for said County John Dockstader of the Town of Palatine, County and State aforesaid, who being first duly sworn according to law deposes and says that he is 86 years of age that he was well acquainted with John VanAntwerpen who was a private in the Revolutionary War and whose widow Rachel Vanantwerpen named in the annexed affidavit applies for a pension or rather sets forth the services of her said husband. That the said Vanantwerpen served in said War in Capt. John Davis (1) Company of Col. Frederick Fisher's Regiment until the battle of Oriskana. The first service was in the latter part of June or beginning of July 1775, occupied 8 days and was done in the Town of Johnstown at Caughnawaga according to the direction of the Committee of Tryon County. In September of the same year was ordered out by Captain John Davis to guard against the tories who collected at Johnson's Hall and served 7 days at different times during the same year there were more meetings of the Militia but I cannot now recollect to specify the times or places.

In the 1776, in the month of January, Capt. John Davis Company was ordered to meet at Caughnawaga with Col. Fisher's Regiment, and was marched to Johnson's Hall, Johnstown, under command of Gen. Philip Schuyler (2)where Sir John Johnson (3) surrendered his arms & the said Vanantwerpen served there 7 days. That in the months of April & May of this same year, said Vanantwerpen was ordered out in Capt. John Davis Company and served in different places at Johnstown, Albany Bush & Scotch Bush in search of Tories 21 days.

That in months of June and part of July Capt. John Davis Compan6y was ordered out to the protection of the inhabitants of Bowman's Creek, Groats Tavern and scouting parties when the said Vanantwerpen served 22 days. That in the year 1777 Col. Fisher ordered out a detachment of Militia to Balstown said Vanantwerpen served therein 8 days under Lieut. Van Brocklin (4) who had command of part of Capt. Abraham Veeder's Company. That in the month of July of the same year said Vanantwerpen went with a scouting party from Johnstown to Fort Miller, served 14 days under command of a Sergeant whose name I cannot recollect—

In the month of August 1777 the whole of Col. F. Fisher's Regiment was ordered out and marched to Oriskana, said Vanantwerpen was in the battle of Oriskana in said Regiment in the company of Captain John Davis who was there killed and thinks Vanantwerpen was out then about three weeks.

In September & October of the same year a part of Capt. Abraham Veeder's Company was ordered to Saratoga under command of Lieut Gerrit Van Brocklin said Vanantwerpen then served with him six weeks—In the year 1778 was ordered out by Captain Abraham Veeder to march to Sacondaga in the month of May where the said Vanantwerpen under command of said Veeder was 7 days at work building a blockhouse.

In the month of June said Vanantwerpen was again ordered out to guard the block house at Sacondaga under command of Capt. John Fisher (5) who had a detachment of Militia and served 30 days—**and further that as near as I can now remember the said Vanantwerpen was again ordered out in Capt. Veeder's Company and marched to Canajoharie, Fort Plain and Fort Plank and there served 19 days**, and also that in October of the year 1778 the said Vanantwerpen was ordered out to Cherry Valley when it was burned by Major Butler, (6) and served then 7 days in Capt. Veeder Company. (Signed) John Docksteter

I certify that I have been acquainted with John Docksteter for more than twenty years last past that he is a credible person and that this affidavit is entitled to full credit. Myndert Starin, Comm. of Deeds &c.

State of New York
County of Montgomery.

John V. Veeder of the town of Mohawk state and County aforesaid being duly sworn says that he is now of the age of seventy four years past that he was well acquainted with John Vanantwerpen in the revolutionary war and with Rachel his wife and was present when they were married by the Rev. Thomas Romyne in my father's house it was in the fall of the year after the expedition of Col. Willett to Oswego (7) to the best of my Recollection on the 22 day of Novem'r but I am not positive to the day of the month but I am positive it was in the year 1783 and no [know] this Rachel Vanantwerpen who now applies for a pension to be the widow of the said John Vanantwerpen who died about ten years since the said Rachel having lived in my fathers house in the war of the Revolution for more than six years, and knew her said husband was a soldier of the Revolutionary War served in the militia and also in a company of Rangers Commanded by Capt. Christian Getman (8) for a Term of 9 months as I then was informed and believe that in the year 1780 the said John Vanantwerpen was takeing a prisoner on the 22 day of May by Sir John Johnson (9) from Canada in or near the house of John Veeder's where a number of Militia were collected he was takeing in arms could not resist the enemy who were two strong and was carried to Canada remained a prisoner till late in the fall or the beginning of the winter when he make his escape from the enemy together with another prisoner Joseph Scot (10) when they both returned again to the Mohawk River. (Signed) John V. Veeder (11)

Subscribed & Sworn to before me this 26th day of September 1837. Myndert Starin, Comm. of Deeds &c.

Additional notes for VanAntwerp, John

His name appears on a list of applicants for invalid pension returned by the district Court for the District of New York, submitted to the House of Representatives by the Secretary of War on April 25, 1794, and printed in the American State Papers, Class 9, page 95.

Rank: Private

Regt: Col. Visscher's

Disability: Wounded in his left heel in an action with some Indians.

When and where disabled: Aug 7, 1777, Oriskie.

Residence: Mohawk Town

Remarks: There are no militia rolls in this office.

Evidence transmitted by the District Court incomplete. Physicians declare that his wound is not injurious. Disability not proved to be the effect of known wounds. No proof when he left the eservice. No proof of a continuance of disability.

Rachel VanAntwerp applied for the pension of her said deceased husband John VanAntwerp on October 31, 1838, while a resident of the Town of Johnstown, Fulton County and was 75 years old.

She states her husband died April 10, 1827.

On June 26, 1839, a daughter, Catharine Coughnet presents from the family bible a record of the marriage of John and Rachel which had been cut out of the bible. "John Van Antwerp, Rachel Allen was married 22 of November 1783."

The following are births known of children for John & Rachel:

Hester born October 19, 1784 and baptized on November 12, 1784, Dutch Reformed Church of Caughnawaga. Baptism Book, page 70.

Johannis baptized July 16, 1786, Dutch Reformed Church of Caughnawaga Baptism Book, page 81.

Johannis born May 17, 1787, baptized June 17, 1787, Dutch Reformed Church of Caughnawaga Baptism Book, page 85.

In the Wills of Montgomery County Book 57, page 268, a will of John VanAntwerp is dated March 28, 1827 and probated on June 4, 1827.

It lists wife Rachel, sons Abraham, Tunis, and Daniel, daughters Caty, Hester, Nelly, Polly, Rachel, and Jane.

Executors are sons Daniel and Tunis. Witnesses are Barent H. Vrooman, Richard Horning and Harmanus VanDusen.

End Notes—W.19897—John VanAntwerp

1. John Davis was appointed Captain on August 26, 1775 of the second company in Colonel Frederick Visscher's Third Regiment of Tryon County Militia.

2. Major General Philip Schuyler of the Continental Army.

3. Sir John Johnson, son of Sir William Johnson lived at Johnson Hall, Johnstown until May of 1776 when he fled to Canada with several of his tenants. Johnson in June of 1776 raised a regiment of loyalists known as the King's Royal Regiment of New York. During the War of Independence they were active against the Americans in the Mohawk and Schoharie Valleys.

4. Garret S. VanBrocklin was an Ensign in Captain Davis' company. Captain Davis was killed at the Battle of Oriskany on August 6, 1777 and the company was then commanded by First Lieutenant Abraham Veeder. In 1778, Veeder was appointed captain, Nicholas Dockstader as first lieutenant, Garret S. VanBrocklin as second

lieutenant, and Dirck Potman (Richard Putman) as ensign. They were all commissioned on March 8, 1781.

5. John Visscher (brother of Colonel Visscher) was appointed captain on August 26, 1775 of the fourth company in Colonel Visscher's Regiment.

6. Captains Walter Butler and Joseph Brant destroyed Cherry Valley on November 11, 1778. Butler's rank was captain in Butler's Ranger commanded by his father Lieutenant-Colonel John Butler.

7. Colonel Marinus Willett's expedition of capture Fort Oswego was in February of 1783.

8. John is listed as enlisting as a private in Captain Christian Getman's Second Company of Tryon County Rangers on August 14, 1776. The company was discharged on March 27, 1777. There is a notation on one of the muster rolls that he had been paid £ 9. . 5. . 3. FROM: Revolutionary War Rolls 1775-1783, Roll 74, folder 103, National Archives, Washington, D.C.

9. Frederick Sammons in his deposition on May 20, 1837 who also had been captured on May 22, 1780, relates the following: "In the year 1780 the 22d day of May Col. John Johnson came from Canada with 6 or 700 British Torys & Indians to destroy the Country when VanAntwerpen was taken prisoner with myself & Tyed with a strong rope and put under a British guard the same day the Indians by leave of the Colo. came and took VanAntwerpen out of the guard & put him under there (sic their) own Guard. I saw him the nex (sic) morning with the Indians painted life an Indian & 8 days afterwards the Indians separated from the British when I saw him the last some tim elate in the fall of the same year I heard he had made his Escape from Montreal in Company with one Joseph Scott who was also a prisoner & further I know not."

10. Lieutenant Benjamin Deline and Joseph Scott were lioving at Johnson Hall and were captured by Johnson on May 22, 1780. Both men were from captain John Littel's (Little) company in Colonel Visscher's Regiment.
11. John Dockstader and Veeder both served in Captain Veeder's Company in Colonel Visscher's Regiment.

Pension Application for John B. Veeder

R.10927

State of New York

County of Schenectada SS.

On this 13th day of October one thousand eight hundred and thirty seven personally appeared before me Samuel W. Jones- -First Judge of the Court of Common Pleas in and for the Court of Common Pleas in and for said County John B. Veeder a resident of the town of Providence in the County of Saratoga in said State aged seventy six years and upwards who being first duly sworn according to law doth on his oath make the following Declaration in order to obtain the benefit of the Act of Congress passed 7 June 1832.

He was born in the township of Schenectada in the now County of Schenectada in said State on the sixth day of November one thousand seven hundred and sixty. He age is recorded in his family bible.

He was living in the said township of Schenectada when he entered the service of the United States. He lived there about fourteen years after leaving the service and then removed to said Town of Providence where he now resides.

He entered the service of the United States under the following named officers and served as herein stated.

He this Declarant in the fall of the year 1779, this Declarant believes in the month of September & October in said year was drafted to serve with a Detachment of Militia from the District of Schenectada at Fort Plank and Stone Arabia and marched with said Detachment to said Fort,

where he served pursuant to such draft for the term of one week at least. This Detachment was commanded by Major Myndert Wemple (1) and the names of his officers in this engagement were Captains Thomas B. Bancker, Lieutenant John B. Vrooman and Aaron or Arent Vedder Second Lieutenant, Ensign Freeman B. Schermerhorn, Adjutant John Lansing and others whose names are not now recollected. **After serving said time of one week at Fort Plank aforesaid this declarant was ordered and marched with a like detachment to Stone Arabia, or Fort Paris where he served under the aforenamed officers for the term of three weeks.**

In the month of June in 1779 he this Declarant served with a Detachment of militia from said District of Schenectada for the term of at least twelve days and this Declarant thinks fourteen days with said Detachment of Militia at Sacondaga under General George Clinton (2) & said Captain Bancker and together with a detachment of Continental troops were engaged in erecting a blockhouse.

In the spring of the year 1780 when the enemy devastated the Mohawk Valley he was on duty with a like detachment and as this Declarant believes under command of Captain Bancker aforesaid & marched on this occasion to Caughnawaga (3) & then returned to Fort Hunter where he performed garrison duty for the term of two weeks.

He this Declarant served for about four or five days with a detachment of Militia and Indians and marched to Beaverdam for the purpose of apprehending a party of Tories there concealed. This occurred in April 1780 & the officers who had charge of this expedition were Major Wemple and said Lieutenant Vedder.

He served with a like detachment for a term of two days and marched to Helderburg in the month of June or July 1780 under command of said Captain Bancker.

He served for the term of one day sometime in the summer of the year 1780 with a small detachment of Militia to the City of Albany to guard some prisoners to said city from Schenectada aforesaid. This Declarant cannot remember who was the Captain of the guard.

This Declarant served with other members of the Militia belonging to the Regiment of said Col. Wemple during the years 1777, 1778, 1779, & 1780 in performing patrol or garrison duty at Schenectada. The then town of Schenectada was at that time surrounded with Pickets and block houses and there were two grand houses within the bounds of the town.

This Declarant took his turn in serving as such guard during the year 1777 for the time of one week as a substitute for others he being at that time only 17 years of age. The captains of the guard where named he recollects were John Clute and John Vrooman. His term came during the years 1778, 1779 & 1780 about once a fortnight & sometimes two or three days in succession but this Declarant cannot specify on what particular days he served. He was called upon to perform such duty as often as other numbers of said militia when not ordered away on distant expeditions. He engaged in said patrol or garrison duty at Schenectady during the year 1778 in his own behalf for the term of not exceeding one week. In the year 1779 for a[t] least fifteen days; in the year 1780 at least twenty days—under the Captains of the guard before named & others different and other officers of the said Regiment.

In the latter part of the month of July or about the beginning of August 1780 (4) he this Declarant marched with a detachment of Militia from said District to Fort Plain. On this occasion the Canajoharie settlements were destroyed by the enemy. They followed the enemy towards Fort Plain & there remained on duty a few days. The whole period of time he was on duty in this engagement was at least three weeks. The following are the names of the officers who had command of this detachment. Colonel Wemple, Major Wemple, Major Swits, Captain Bancker aforesaid Captain Abraham Oothout (5) and nearly all the other officers of said Regiment of Colonel Abraham Wemple.

In the month of June 1781 he this Declarant served with a like detachment at Fort Plank under said Captain Bancker for the term of one week or ten days from thence he was ordered to Stone Arabia where he performed garrison duty one week under command of one Major VanBuren. (6)

At this time Ballston was destroyed by the enemy this Declarant marched with a like Detachment to Ballston under command of said Captain Bancker where he performed garrison duty for a few days & served in this engagement for the term of two weeks.

In and for the year 1781 this Declarant enlisted and served in the volunteer Company of Artillery commanded by Captain John Crousehorn in Schenectada aforesaid. This company was comprised of fifteen men and were particularly charged with the custody of the cannon belonging to said Regiment of Colonel Wemple aforesaid, to fire alarms on the approach of the enemy and on other occasions said company also engaged as occasion required in performing garrison duty at Schenectada aforesaid and at other places. He served in said company during said year 1781 discharging [?] duty at the Schenectada garrison aforesaid for a term in the whole exceeding one month and when not on garrison duty was regularly every week drilled and reviewed by the officers of said Regiment who were for the time being at Schenectada aforesaid.

Late in the fall of the year 1780 he marched with a detachment of Militia about twenty five miles up the Mohawk River for a place opposite Caughnawaga on the south side of said river. Colonel Wemple aforesaid and Major Wemple had the command of said detachment.

He this Declarant served with a detachment of seven militia served for the term of three days under command of Lieutenant J. H. Peek [or Peck] & John Thornton (7) in an expedition to Milton and Lake Desolation in pursuit of a noted Tory Joseph Bettis who was afterwards apprehended & hung in the year 1782 in the City of Albany.

The following are the names of some of the regular officers whom he knew, or who were with the troops where he served, and such continental and militia regiments or companies with which he served or as he can recollect, viz: Colonel Marinus Willett, General Sullivan, Adjutant Jellis A. Fonda, General Gansevoort, Colonel VanDyck, Captain Fink, Col. Clock, Captain John Mynderse, Capt. Jess VanSlyck (8) & all the other captains of said Regiment of Col. Wemple.

He never received any written discharge from the service.

He has no documentary evidence and knows of no person whose testimony he can procure who can testify to his service except those whose testimony is hereto annexed.

The following are the names of persons to whom he is known in his present neighborhood, and who can testify as to his character for veracity and their belief of his services as a soldier of the revolution, to wit John DeGraff, Richard VanVranken, John J. Shew, Jacob Shew, Nathaniel Wescot & John Fay.

He hereby relinquishes every claim whatever, to a pension or annuity except the present, and declares that his name is not on the pension roll of the agency of any State. (Signed) John B. Veeder

Subscribed and sworn to the day and year first aforesaid. S. W. Jones, First Judge of Schenectady County.

End Notes—John B. Veeder--R.10927

1. Second Major Myndert Vrooman and Captain Thomas Bancker's Company were in Colonel Abraham Wemple's Regiment of Albany County Militia.

2. It was Brigadier General James Clinton who had ordered the Sacondaga Blockhouse to be built in April of 1779. Colonel Frederick Visscher with a detachment of the Third Regiment of Tryon County Militia and a detachment of the

Fifth New York Continental Regiment were also there in helping to build the blockhouse.

3. Caughnawaga and the surrounding area were destroyed on May 22, 1780 by Sir John Johnson and his British and Indian Forces.

4. The area is present day Village of Fort Plain and the Town of Minden, Montgomery County. Captain Joseph Brant destroyed this area on August 2, 1780.

5. First Major Abraham Swits and Captain Abraham Oothout (Oathout, etc.) were from Colonel Wemple's Regiment.

6. There were two different Major VanBurens. Major Cornelius VanBuren of the Fourth Regiment and Major Herman VanBuren of the Seventh Regiment. Both were Albany County Regiments.

7. Jacobus Peek (Peake, Peck, etc.) and John Thornton were both lieutenants in Colonel Wemple's Regiment. John's name also appears on a roll in Captain Jesse VanSlyck's Company also in Colonel Wemple's Regiment.

8. Major General John Sullivan, Brigadier General Peter Gansevoort. Gansevoort was colonel of the Third New York Continental Regiment from November 21, 1776 to January 1, 1781. March 26, 1781 he was appointed to the First Brigade of Albany County Militia because General Abraham Ten Broeck had resigned because of his health. Lieutenant-Colonel Cornelius VanDyck of the First New York Continental Regiment, Captain Andrew Finck of the First New York, Colonel Jacob Klock of the Second Regiment of Tryon County Militia and Captain John Mynderse (Mynderson) of Colonel Wemple's Regiment. Marinus Willett had been Lieutenant-Colonel of the Third New York and Fifth New York, and colonel of a regiment of New York State Levies 1781-1783. Jellis A. Fonda had been an ensign in Wemple's Regt and a lieutenant and

adjutant in Willett's Levies 1781-1782 and captain November 1782-November 1783.

Pension Application for Jacob Yonger, Youger, Youker, Jukker, Uker, Yuger, Yuker, Yougher, Jucker

S.11925

Jacob was awarded a pension of $46.41 per annum, Certificate of Pension issued the 9th day of July 1833.

State of New York

Montgomery County

On this 22 day of September in the year eighteen hundred & thirty two personally appeared in open court before the Judges of the Court of Common Pleas held at the Court House in Johnstown now sitting Jacob Youger of the Town of Openheim [Oppenheim] in the County of Montgomery & State of New York aged seventy five years next October, who being first duly sworn according to law doth, on his oath make the following declaration in order to obtain the benefit of the Act of Congress passed June 7th 1832.

That he was born in the town of Palatine (now called Openheim) in the County of Montgomery & State of New York on the 26th day of October in the year 1757—That he resided there during the Revolutionary War & also since that time until the present.—That he entered the service of the United States about the first of June as near as he can recollect in the year 1777 under the command of Captain Samuel Gray (1) in Colonel Klock's Regiment of Militia—That he enlisted at this time for the term of six months to act as a Minute Man—(2) ready to go when called for by the Officers—That he was ordered to march to German Flatts to guard Fort Herkimer—That while there about three hundred Indians & Tories from Canada commenced an attack upon the Fort & after a few hours fight they retreated--& they followed them about three miles when they again returned to the Fort—he thinks there were no men lost at this time—that he remained at the Fort about six weeks when he returned home about the middle of August following—that while he pretended to stay at home there was not scarcely a week but he was called out continually on alarms & for scouts, some times one two three days & sometime whole weeks at a time of which he kept no regular account—but so often was he called upon that he could do nothing else until his six months expired which was on or about the last of November of that same year.

That soon after this time expired and thinks about the first of December following he was drafted & served most of the time under the command of Captain Christian House (3) & still under the command of Colonel Klock until the close of the war:-- That the company to which he belonged was divided into two classes—one class serving two weeks & then the other class would release them when they would serve two weeks & so alternately relieving each other every two weeks—That he was ordered to guard Remus Snyder's Fort between the Little Falls & Fairfield—That he served as above stated sometimes under the command of Christian House, sometimes under the Command of Henry Hoover (4) who was also Captain until in the Spring on the first day of March 1782 (5) when he was drafted out of the Fort on a Scouting party to Yanky Bush about three miles from the Fort— That he had been frequently drafted but does not recollect the particulars of any except this time—and the reason he particularly recollects this is because he was taken on the second day of March in the year 1782 a prisoner by a company of about fifty men including Tories & Indians—That he & one George Adle were alone on the scout when they were taken prisoners & led to their camp when they were detained by some of the enemy while the others went into the settlement & took nineteen others among them were John Boyer, John House & the names of the others he cannot recollect—That after the Enemy had returned with their nineteen prisoners they moved off to Canada where all were taken except one George Adle who ran away—That they landed first at Buck's Island & from there they were taken to Montreal—That he was kept there until about the latter part of the month of October following when he and one other, whose name he cannot recollect ran away from there & returned, the same way that they were taken, home—being in all about eight months.—(6)

That after he returned he did not again enter the service until the latter part of August in the following year when he again went out in pursuit of John Butler, (7) [Walter Butler] who was then on his retreat from Johnstown (8) & under the Command of Christian House & was absent a few days—That he does not recollect the names of any other officers except those above named,--That he never received a discharge and has no documentary evidence of his services—That he is known in the neighborhood where he resides by Jacob J. Failing & John J. Failing, who will testify to his character for veracity—good behavior—and reputed services as soldier of the Revolution—That he knows of no person who can testify to his service & being taken a prisoner except Jacob J. Failing whose affidavit is hereto annexed—That he hereby relinquishes every claim whatever to a pension or annuity except the present and declares that his name is not on the pension Roll of the Agency of any State—That no Clergyman resides in his neighborhood whose certificate he can obtain. (Signed with his mark) Jacob Youger

Sworn to and Subscribed the day & year above written. Geo: D. Ferguson, Clerk.

State of New York
Montgomery County SS

Personally appeared this 29th day of January A.D. 1833 before me the undersigned a Justice of the Peace in the Town of Oppenheim in the said County, Jacob Younger who being duly sworn says that by reason of old age & the subsequent loss of his memory he cannot swear positively as to the precise length of his services but according to the best of his recollection he served the following tours of service & not less than the periods mentioned below & in the following grade—viz:--

That he and others enlisted for six months as minute men so called then & were to hold themselves in readiness to serve when required in the company whereof Samuel Gray was Capt in the Regt of Infantry of the Revolutionary Army in the State of New York whereof Jacob Klock was called the Col that he served in said Company as a private from June 1, 1777 to July 12, 1777 for one month & twelve days during said term of six months as follows on a tour of service—that he in said company commanded by said Capt. Gray were marched from the Town of Palatine where he resided when he entered said service to Fort Herkimer where he & said Company were stationed for said one month & twelve days when they returned home—said Company belonged according to his recollection to the Regt but cannot be positive.

That he also served during the last mentioned six months on a tour of service as a private in same company & Regt under same officers last mentioned from Augt 2d 1777 to Augt 16th 1777 for fourteen days as follows that he & said Company were marched from the Town of Palatine to Fort "Loucks" on Stonearabia in the same town & were stationed there during said fourteen days when they returned home—that when he entered on the last tour he resided in the now Town of Oppenheim in said County--& that he recd only a verbal discharge.

That he also during said Six months served on a tour of service as a private in the same Company & Regt & under same officers above mentioned from 20 Augt 1777 to 20 September 1777 for one month as follows & that he & said Company were marched from then Town of Palatine to Fort Plank (so called) about four miles westwardly from Fort Plain in the Town of Minden & that said Forts are sometimes confounded but that there were two Forts of the names aforesaid the Former Fort some miles westerly in same Town from Fort Plain—that he & said Company were marched to

said Fort Plank &c were there stationed for one month--& then returned home, that he resided in the said Town of Oppenheim in said County when he entered on last mentioned tour of duty & further says that the minute men as he understood were only obliged to serve & keep themselves in readiness when they were required—that they enlisted for 6 months & during that time he served the aforesaid three tours of service for the periods aforesaid respectfully, which said tours were the only important ones he can recollect so as to give a detail thereof.—

That he served also as a private soldier in the company whereof Christian House was Capt & in the Regt whereof Jacob Klock was Col. From May 1st 1778 to 16th May 1778 for sixteen days as follows—that he was drafted out of said company & was marched to Fort Herkimer & there stationed guarding said Fort for said period last mentioned—that one Herkimer (9) (whose Christian name he cannot recollect) commanded there said Fort & was an officer & according to his recollection of the rank of Captain—that while in said Fort a party of Tories & Indians passed by said Fort & fired upon the Fort & was returned from the Fort—but the tories & Indians retired & were pursued by him & others in the Fort for some days without being able to come up with them -- & they returned to the Fort—that some soldiers belonging to the revolutionary Army came to the said Fort after the battle & went also in pursuit of the Indians & Tories—

That about 600 men (10) followed the Indians as aforesaid in order to over take them—but also commanded the whole body of men he cannot recollect.—but he was under the Command of said Herkimer—that the Indians returned as supposed to Canada—when the men who came to the Fort after the battle or skirmish went away from said Fort Eastward -- & where to he cannot recollect—

That when last tour of service he resided in the now Town of Oppenheim in said county--& cannot more particularly state last mentioned services—that said Company & Regt belonged to the infantry of the militia of the State of New York of the revolutionary Army—that Capt House did not accompany those drafted out of his Company-- That he also served as a private in the same Company & Regt last mentioned of which Company Christian House was Capt & Jacob Klock Col of said Regt from first day of June 1778 to fifth day of June 1778 for four days as follows that he was ordered out by his Commanding officers—that the said Company went—that he & said Company were marched from the Town of Oppenheim in said County to Remer—Snyder's Bush in the now Town of Manheim in Herkimer County—thence to Fairfield in same County--& were marched back to Remer— Snyder's Bush (11)—that the Indians & Tories had at or near Fairfield Killed some of the Inhabitants & taken others prisoners—that his Capt (House) Commanded said Company & Col Klock said Regt—that the Regt were also on this tour of duty—that he served said four days when he was discharged verbally & returned home—that he resided in the now Town of Oppenheim in Montgomery Co., when he entered on last mentioned tour of duty.

That he also served as a private in the same company & Regt aforesaid under the same officers from 10th November 1778 to 16th November 1778 for six days as follows—that he was ordered into this service by his commanding officers—that the company & Regt marched to Cherry Valley (12) & arrived there the day after the massacre of the inhabitants of that place, by the Tories & Indians—that he saw many of the inhabitants that were killed & assisted in putting the dead bodies on wagon to take some to the Fort at said place—that Jacob Klock commanded said Regt on this tour of duty – that when he entered last mentioned tour of duty he resided in the now Town of Oppenheim in said County.

That he also served as a private in the Company & Regt last mentioned commanded by the same officers last mentioned from the 25th of April 1779 to the tenth day of May 1779 for sixteen days at least as follows—that he & part of said Company were drafted on this tour of service—that Conradt Timmerman (13) an Ensign in said Company Commanded him & those that were drafted as last mentioned—that they were marched from now Town of Oppenheim to Stone Arabia to Fort "Loucks" in said County of Montgomery & were there stationed for said period doing duty as a soldier—for said sixteen days—then were discharged & returned home—that when he entered last tour of service he resided in the Town of Oppenheim County of Montgomery—

That he also served as a private in the same Company & Regt last mentioned under the same officers thereto belonging as aforesaid from first day of June 1779 to sixteenth day of June 1779 for sixteen days as follows—that he & others of said Company was drafted on this tour of duty—that Conradt Timmerman his Ensign Commanded him & said party that were drafted on this occasion—that they were marched from the now Town of Oppenheim in Montgomery Co., to Fort Plain where they were stationed for said period last mentioned—according to his recollection Capt Gross (14) whom (he thinks) he saw at this Fort commanded said Fort but cannot swear positively & Cannot recollect the name of any other officer he saw at said fort, tho' there were other militia officers there, that he served said sixteen days as aforesaid & when he entered one this tour of service he resided in the now Town of Oppenheim in Montgomery Co.—

That he also served as a private soldier in the same Company & Regt aforesaid last mentioned under same officers from sixth day of July A.D. 1779 to twentieth day of July 1779 for fourteen days as follows—Viz—that he & others of said Company were drafted out of said Company & Regt.—that they went from Town of Oppenheim, Montgomery County., were marched to Remer Snyder's Bush where was a small Fort & while in Fort he was commanded by Capt Henry Hoover who commanded said Fort—that he was stationed at said Fort during said fourteen days doing duty as a private—that he was verbally discharged & when he entered last mentioned service he resided in the now Town of Oppenheim in said County of Montgomery that his Capt (House) did not accompany them on this service—

That he served also as a private in the Company aforesaid whereas Captain House was Capt in the Regt whereof Jacob Klock was Col. from the fifteenth day of August 1779 to the thirtieth day of August 1779 for fifteen days as follows—that he & some others out of said Company were drafted & were marched again [to] Remer Snyder's Fort in the now Town of Manheim County of Herkimer & that he & those drafted were stationed in said fort was Commanded by John Keyser (15) a militia Captain under whom he served at said Fort for the period last aforesaid— that none of the commissioned officers of Capt. House's Company accompanied them in this tour of service—that he served as a private for said fifteen days & then returned home that when he entered last mentioned service he resided in the now Town of Oppenheim Montgomery County.

That he also served as a private in said Company whereof Christian House was Capt in Regt whereof Jacob Klock was Col. of the militia of the State of New York from Sept 6, 1779 to Sept 9, 1779 for three days as follows—

That he & about fifteen others of said Company were drafted on a scouting party – that they marched up the East Canada Creek for a whole day & next day they took two Indians prisoners who were heavily laden with fur—that they took the Indians to Col. Klock's house & assisted them in carrying their Packs when they arrived at the Cols House the Indians were discharged as on enquiry it was ascertained that they were friendly Indians, who were going to Albany to sell their fur—that he served said three days on said scouting party as aforesaid & when he entered he resided in said Town of Oppenheim.

That he also served as a private in same Company & Regt last mentioned under same officers from Sept 13th to Sept 15th

1779 for two days as follows & that the said company or those not in service then together with were ordered out by his Commanding officers into the service—that the Captain accompanied said Company—that they were marched to "Kringsbush" & returned home next day—that a building was burned at said place which caused them to go out supposing at the time that the Indians had done it--but it turned out that a young woman had set fire to the building—that he resided in the same Town of Oppenheim when he entered in last mentioned service.

That he also served as a private in the Company whereof Christian House was Capt. in the Regt whereof Jacob Klock was Col. from the first day of March 1780 to 2d day of March 1780 for two days as follows—that he was drafted with others of said Company & were marched by the said Capt on said first day of March 1780 to Remer Snyder's Fort that the day after to wit on 2d March he & one Adel were drafted out of said Fort on a scout --& same day they while on scout were taken prisoners—that he remained a Prisoner until twenty eight day of Octr 1780 for seven months & twenty six days being the whole time of his being a prisoner when he ran away & returned home—that as this tour of service & the above facts herein stated are correct according to his recollection he desires his original declaration being incorrect as to the dates of the facts herein stated—That he resided in the now Town of Oppenheim aforesaid when he entered last service & being a prisoner were made by the person who drew his said original declaration.—

That he also served as a private the year following his return from imprisonment last above mentioned in same officers commanding from 23d of Augt 1781—25 Augt 1781 for two days—that said Company & himself joined Col. Willet in pursuit after the Indians & Tories on their retreat from the battle at Johnstown—that Walter Butler was killed near the Canada Creek—that he joined said Willet troops after the battle—that he resided in the said Town of Oppenheim when he entered last mentioned service & further says that he was on other short tours of duty not mentioned—claim only a Pension for his services & time of Imprisonment aforesaid, & detailed—If the time of his imprisonment cannot be allowed, the same will then be deducted—that he can produce no other or further proof then that contained in his original proceedings – that when he entered on aforesaid service he resided in the now Town of Oppenheim County of Montgomery aforesaid & has stated his said services as fully as he can recollect same--& further says not-- (Signed with his mark) Jacob Youker

Sworn & subscribed this 29th day of January A.D. 1833 before me. Ashbel Loomis Justice of the Peace.

End Notes—S.11925—Jacob Youker

1. The Tryon County Battalion of the Minute Man was authorized to be raised on September 19, 1775. George Herkimer was appointed colonel and Samuel Gray as the Adjutant (the Adjutant usually held a commission of a lieutenant or ensign). So far no company muster rolls have been found for the Minute Men Battalion. If Jacob served in this unit it would have been in 1775 or until the middle of 1776. On June 5, 1776 New York's Provincial Congress ordered "1st That the distinction between Minute Men and Common Militia which seems to be a consequence of the aforesaid Resolve of the Continental Congress be henceforth abolished, that thereby the Militia of the Colony may be again reduced to one Common mass." 2dly That therefore all the Commissions for Minute Officers be forthwith recalled and that every private be placed under his proper Militia Officer, leaving each Regiment to be Officered according to the Mode prescribed, that is to say— Those under the degree of Field Officers by Election of the privates & those above that Degree by the appointment of the Provincial Congress". FROM: Documents Relating to

the Colonial History of the State of New York ed. Berthold Fernow, Vol. XV, State Archives, Vol I, Weed, Parsons and Company Printers, P. 105, Albany, N.Y. 1887.

2. Forts Herkimer and Dayton were attacked on September 17, 1778 and again on July 15, 1782.

3. Christian House was appointed on August 26, 1775 Captain of the Seventh Company in Colonel Jacob Klock's Second Regiment of Tryon County Militia. This is the Company that Jacob would have served in 1775 except when on minute man duty. There are two pay receipts for Jacob for service in Colonel Klock's Regiment no. 2164 £ 2. . 16. . 10 2/3 and no. 2134 £1. . 1. .

4. Henry Huber was a Captain in Colonel Peter Bellinger's Fourth Regiment of Tryon County Militia. Captain Huber was taken prisoner at the Battle of Oriskany on August 6, 1777. He was paroled and returned home in 1778.

5. Jacob was taken prisoner on April 3, 1780 with George Attle, (Eadel, Edel, etc.) who later escaped and returned home by April 25, 1780.

6. This part is fabricated. He enlisted into the British service on April 3, 1780 in the First Battalion of the King's Royal Regiment of New York which was commanded by Sir John Johnson. John Carter and his father were also taken prisoner in the April 3 raid, and in Book 1 of Don't Shoot is his pension application on pp 69-77, it is an interesting account of the raid. Jacob's enlistment is in "Casuals of the KRR NY since formation, Point Clair, 17 May 1783", includes names, Dates of Enlistment, Death, Discharge or desertion, MG 21 B158, pp 208-210. Gov. Frederick Haldimand Papers, British Museum, England. Jacob is listed as deserting on October 26, 1780 and also a John Cogdon is listed as deserting on the same date. Cogdon had deserted on May 22, 1780 from Colonel Goose VanSchaick's First New York Continental Regiment. The

First New York was stationed at Fort Schuyler in 1779, and 1780. By May of 1780 the morale was so bad that about two dozen men deserted on the same night including the Drum Major Henry Keyser. Cogdon was a private in Captain Andrew Fink's Third Company and is listed in the November 1780 Company Muster Roll as returning to the Company on October 6, 1780. Cogdon served to the end of the War and received 500 acres of Bounty Land for his service in Township 5 (Camillus) Lot 51 on July 7, 1790.

7. Captain Walter Butler son of Lieutenant Colonel John Butler was killed in the skirmish at West Canada Creek on October 30, 1780.

8. On October 25, 1781, a battle was fought at Johnstown between American troops under Lieutenant-Colonel Commandant Marinus Willett and British forces under Major John Ross and Captain Butler.

9. George Herkimer had been appointed Captain in Colonel Bellinger's Regiment on August 26, 1775 but by the end of the year he was Cashiered for conduct unbecoming an officer. He was also the Colonel of the Minute Men but after June of 1776 he would have been just a private soldier in Colonel Bellinger's Regiment. George may have been at Fort Herkimer as he lived within a couple of miles from the fort.

10. This added information on the attack of Fort Herkimer tends to lean towards the July 15, 1782 raid led by Captain George Singleton of the King's Royal Regiment of New York and Captain Joseph Brant. Major Andrew Finck of Willett's Regiment did arrive with more troops and renewed the pursuit of the raiders.

11. Remesnyders' Bush, Snyder's Bush etc. was raided at least twice during the War of Independence. A block

house was built there to protect the grist mill owned by Henry Rumsnider as he spelled it later.

12. Cherry Valley was destroyed on November 11, 1778 by Captains Walter Butler and Joseph Brant.

13. Henry Zimmerman was commissioned ensign on June 25, 1778 in Captain House's Company and Conrad Zimmerman was serving as a sergeant in the same company. On March 4, 1780, Henry Zimmerman was commissioned the second lieutenant and Conrad Zimmerman as the ensign in Captain House's Company.

14. Lawrence Gros was not appointed Captain until April 27, 1781. On that date he was appointed Captain in Willett's Regiment of Levies. Gros served in Captain John Ruff's (or Roof) Company as lieutenant which were attached to Colonel Klock's regiment in 1779. Ruff's company appears to be a company of exempts. One year they were attached to Klock's Regiment and one year they were attached to Colonel Samuel Campbell's First Regiment of Tryon County Militia.

15. John Keyser was a Captain in Colonel Klock's regiment. He was taken prisoner on March 15, 1780 and kept a prisoner until he was released on September 3, 1781. FROM: Audited Accounts Vol. A. Page 291, Special Collections and Manuscripts, New York State Library, Albany, NY.

Excerpts from various pensions.

Excerpt from Thomas Campbell's pension application.

Excerpt from John DeGraff's pension application.

Excerpt from John Duesler's pension application.

Excerpt from William Feeter's pension application.

Excerpt from Francis Frederick's pension application.

Excerpt from Lodowick Moyer's pension application.

Excerpt from John VanAntwerp's pension application.

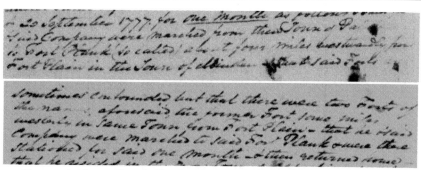

Excerpts from Jacob Youker's pension application where he
addresses the issue of one fort or two forts.

Made in the USA
San Bernardino, CA
14 August 2017